DREAM
QUEST

The Trials, Tribulations, and Triumph of a Prodigal Son

Melvin J. Coleman

ISBN 978-1-63885-610-8 (Paperback)
ISBN 978-1-63885-611-5 (Digital)

Covenant Books, Inc.
11661 Hwy 707
Murrells Inlet, SC 29576
www.covenantbooks.com

To my grandparents, my parents, my children, and grandchildren, big sister Maryann Wade, baby sisters Priscilla and Georgette, and my wife, Michelle (Mémé) Banks (RIH)

ACKNOWLEDGMENTS

I am indebted to all of the people who played a role in helping me to recollect those significant events in my life in order for me to accurately give account and be able to share my experience.

Special thanks to family, Marvin Snipes, David Snipes, Barbara J. Austin, Stella Evans, and Gladys Faulkner (Queen G), my love.

INTRODUCTION

Driven by the desire to be free to explore and experience life as I saw it through my own eyes and to understand the reason why things were as they were in my little world, I yearned for peace at any expense. But how, when, and where would I find it? This was my greatest pain.

I was born on Chicago's west side on Washington Boulevard to my mother Ossie Coleman and my father Edward Coleman. I was one of seven children. I was just a toddler when we moved to the South Side with my six brothers and sisters: James, Maryann, Barbara, Jean, Edward, Howard, and Priscilla. I don't remember much about living with our mom Ossie. As far as I can recall, we always lived at Grandma Joanna's house, our mom's mom.

We lived in a three-story red and white brick building on thirty-fifth and Prairie Street. I think that my brothers James and Edward and my sister Maryann were already grown and had moved from home before we got to Grandma Joanna's house. I learned that my brother Edward was living with my other Grandmother Mittie— my father's mother on Thirty-Fifth and Michigan. Barbara, myself, Howard, and Priscilla remained with Grandma Joanna. Priscilla and I attended Douglas School on Thirty-Third and Calumet Avenue. Howard had a disability from birth and always remained home with Grandma. Barbara, as far as I can remember, was sort of in and out of school mostly and hung out with friends. Grandma was strict and no nonsense in her ways but always made sure we were properly fed, dressed, and cared for. It was very hard for families back then having to rely solely on public aid (ADC) to survive and when fathers weren't allowed to live in the house with their wives and children. If found out, the aid would be cut off. This made it extra hard on families when fathers had to sneak in and out to see and feed their families. Despite all, we were always provided for and never went cold or hungry.

Our families were one of the largest and most well-known on our block. Mothers, fathers, aunts, uncles, brothers, sisters, and cousins, there were just so many of us. There were times when our families would get into it with one of the other families, and it was a sight to behold because we were all like one big family on the block at times, and at other times, it was family squabble time. It would start from the youngest to the oldest on both sides. But no one was ever seriously hurt, and afterward, everything was as if it had never happened.

I recall that time when I wanted a tricycle so bad. I asked and asked and cried and cried to Grandma to buy me a tricycle. She always said, when I get bigger as I was always small for my age, and I had been born with bronchitis and asthma, and once, my parents were told I wouldn't survive. Well, Grandma finally gave in and bought me a brand-new radio flyer tricycle. I couldn't wait to hit the sidewalk after watching all the other kids so long riding up and down on their tricycles, wagons, and bicycles. Now it was my turn to show what I could do. One of my uncles took me and my tricycle downstairs. I got on and Uncle was pushing me along up and down the block. I pleaded with my uncle to let me do it by myself; he finally agreed. I took off peddling as fast as I could; my uncle was shouting to not go so fast! But I had to show off my stuff, and just then, I heard a bump, and next thing, I was flying over the handle bars of my tricycle. Face-first, I hit the sidewalk sliding I managed to get up just as my uncle and other people ran to me. A lot were screaming and hollering, "Poor baby." I didn't feel anything, but I looked down at my T-shirt to wipe the dirt off, and all I saw was blood. And it was dripping from my chin. Just then, someone put a cold towel under my chin, wrapped a blanket around me, and put me in a car. That's the last I remembered until I woke up the next day—all bandaged under my chin. Then I heard one of my uncles say, "How're you doing rough house?" And he said, "This boy is as rough as can be. He never cried one time from that fall and his chin laying wide open. That's old rough house." Grandma kept me home from school for a few days until my stitches healed. Soon, I returned to school, and everything was back to normal. I really had fun at school. In everything I participated in, I was exceptionally good at it.

In class and at play, at recess time, I could swing as high as anybody, run as fast even though I had asthma, and after school, the boys had wrestling at the shelter house. I was quick and fast and could outsmart most of the other boys. I wasn't sad at home but longed for the fun to go on and on, and when I had to be in, I'd look out the window at all the other children running and playing well until dark. I had to be in when the streetlights came on. How I wished that I had the freedom that they had. As night drew on, I could see my older brother James, my cousin Marvin, and others gather across the street on the porch of the building where Grandma's sister, Aunt Gertrude, lived. They were drinking their wine, smoking their cigarettes, and singing. Their voices filled the night, and people would stop and listen. I wanted to be grown like they were, not having to go to school, do chores, and stay out later, late at night with no one to tell you what to do and seemingly not having a care in the world. *That could be the life for me*, I thought.

My father's mother, Mittie, lived on Michigan Avenue, and she would send one of the tenants from her rental flat named Mr. Brown to pick me up from Grandma Joanna's for the weekend on Fridays. After play, just before sunset, I would go in, wash up, and change clothes and wait for Mr. Brown to come across the vacant lot toward Grandma's house. I'd always become nervous as it grew darker outside. I feared, maybe, he wouldn't come. I really looked forward to those weekends over to Grandma Mittie's. She was more lenient with me and sort of let me have my way with just about anything. I'd spend weekends, birthday's, and mainly Christmastime there and parts of the summer vacation. On weekends, I wished that Sunday would never come because I knew at sundown Sunday, it was back home and off to school on Monday morning.

At that time, Priscilla was the baby. She and I were very close. She was very timid, and I always looked out for her. Grandma was very particular about letting her out of her sight for too long except for school and playtime after school. Even then, she was to play where Grandma could keep a watchful eye on her. Well, it was time for another summer vacation, and Mr. Brown came to the house as usual but this time, much earlier than the others. He wanted to talk to Grandma alone, so Priscilla, Howard, and I left the room. All I could think of was, *Maybe, something was wrong, and I wouldn't be going to see Grandma Mittie this time, but what did Priscilla and Howard have to do with it?* I wondered. Later, Grandma called for us to come to the living room. She said that Mr. Brown had come to take the three of us: Howard, Priscilla, and myself to Grandma Mittie's for a special surprise. We were all so glad. On the way, Mr. Brown gave us no clue as to what the surprise was no matter our trying to find out every step of the way.

When we got upstairs, we could hear Grandma Mittie talking to someone. There was a man standing in her doorway with his back to us. Just then, he turned around. It was Dad Edward; he had come home from the navy. I only recognized him by his uniform and from pictures on Grandma Mittie's dresser. I was very young when he left. He hugged us all and said we would go for a ride. I thought maybe on the bus or the El train. I hadn't ridden in cars that much. We all went downstairs holding on to him. We walked across the alley to a small "Tasty Freeze" ice cream stand. He bought us ice cream. Then we walked to the service station next door.

He walked up to a shiny blue car, opened all the doors, and said, "Get in. Let's go shopping."

We rode around for a while, then we went to the Lake Meadows Shopping Center. He told us to get whatever we wanted. We bought some of everything; I don't recall exactly what. We ate hot dogs and candy. It was getting late, so it was time to go back to Grandma Mittie's. We arrived at Grandma's, and Dad walked us upstairs and saw us into the house, hugged us all, and left. Just then, Mr. Brown was ready to take Howard and Priscilla back to Grandma Joanna's. I was staying at Grandma Mittie's for the weekend. Through all the excitement, I hadn't seen or thought of my brother Edward. Grandma Mittie told me that Edward was in "Chicago Parental School" for truant and bad boys but that she goes to visit him often, and he would be coming home soon.

Edward and I had our own room to share. I had my toys, and Edward had his comic books, records, and model cars, planes, and different things he had made in parental school. I had my side of the room, and he had his. I had many toy cowboys, Indians, horses, plus all my army men—so many they would almost stretch the entire hallway. I'd crawl from one end of the hall to the other playing with them. Then Grandma Mittie let me have a cat that I named Panther because it was shiny black all over. I raised it from a kitten. Then as Panther grew and got older, he became more independent going outside and staying for days at a time until one day, he left and never returned.

Grandma explained that's the way of cats. It took me awhile, but I understood and got over it. Sometimes, I dreaded that Sunday had come, and the sun would be setting. That meant that one of my uncles would be coming for me to take me home. I had school and chores until next weekend, but I liked being around my friends and family and all the excitement that happens from time to time, never really a dull day.

Although I enjoyed playing with my friends, I sometimes would go off to myself and just sort of wonder what it would be like if I were grown up and on my own, no one to tell me when to come in the house, when to go to bed, and be able to do what I want when I want. But soon, the daydream would fade as the sun was setting and dark would be coming and it would be "in the house" when the street-lights came on and back to my regular routine of school and chores. But at home with Grandma Joanna were, many times, just as exciting and interesting as she would, in her own way, administer to the sick and destitute who came to her for help and advice. They always had some of the most interesting stories to tell, and some of them I wish I had experienced. Then there was my older brother James who would come by on the watermelon wagon hollering watermelons for sale and watching the people flock out to buy from the horse-drawn wagon. Then I would see some other boys helping on the wagon carrying watermelons to the houses—oh, how I wish I could do that. Brother James would always send a free watermelon to Grandma. I hated to see him leave not knowing when he would come by again.

He very seldom came by the house to visit as he and Grandma didn't get along too well. Every time he came by, I wish I could go with him and learn to drive the horse and sell watermelons. I didn't get to do that too soon, but one day, a man we called Fat Earl came by on his vegetable truck looking for boys to work with him. I asked Grandma if I could. She agreed as long as I was home by sunset. It was great. I was seeing other parts of our neighborhoods I hadn't had

13

occasion to see. I made new friends, and most of all, I was earning my own money and was feeling sort of grown-up and responsible. From here, Grandma let me do more and more things like letting me take Priscilla to church by myself and let me walk us to school by ourselves. Before, we always had to be accompanied by an adult. She even let me get a paper route. Wow, this was really great. I was as big brother now.

My mom and dad were separated at this time, and mom was living with a man by the name of George Dupino; they lived on South Park, about three blocks from Prairie. Priscilla and I would often go and visit mom after school. This man didn't really care for mom's kids as we often heard him say things about us. He had no problem showing it. He and mom had a business selling pastries, hot dogs, candy, etc., out of a station wagon car. He didn't care for Mom giving us things for free or even her paying for it for us. He'd argue with her all the time about it saying that she should let Grandma or the rest of the family pay and that he had to pay for the things. He was really resentful of us.

Soon, they rented a restaurant on Indiana Avenue just a block from where we lived. They had really good business there, and everyone, young and old, came to their restaurant. Just about everyone in the neighborhood knew mom. Later, Mom got pregnant with George's child. It was a girl. They named her Georgette after George's name. She was a pretty baby. I was so happy to have another little sister. Priscilla and I would go to the restaurant just to see and play with her in the back room. We also would come to eat some of the special dishes that mom had cooked. Even then, George would complain she was giving us too much food. She shouldn't let us come and eat there every day. Many times, we'd even overhear him and Mom shouting in the back room, and Mom would come out in tears and tell us we had to go. It was sad to see the way he treated mom. It wasn't so much how he felt about us.

We told Grandma what had happened when we got home. Grandma said that we should stay away from the restaurant and that Mom should leave George because something bad was going to happen one day. She used her favorite phrase when she felt she was right about a thing. She'd say, "Mark my word!" Lo and behold, not long after, we got word that our little sister Georgette was dead. We were told that Mom and George had a physical fight and that George somehow fell on Georgette killing her. George weighed well over three hundred pounds, if anything. I don't recall her funeral or what exactly happened after that.

Well, things went on as normal for the next few months until one weekend, I waited for Mr. Brown to come across the vacant lot to come for me to go to Grandma Mittie's, but he didn't come Friday or Saturday, and I knew he wouldn't come Sunday because I had to be home for school on Monday. I didn't cry, but I was so sad. All I could think of was that maybe he got sick or maybe Grandma Mittie was sick, and he had to stay with her. They always looked out for each other that way. Well, Monday came. I went to school convincing myself there was nothing to be sad about and that he would come this weekend for sure. Then to my surprise, he came during that week. I didn't know what to expect. When he came in, he picked me up and hugged me and said he'd see me in a bit. He wanted to talk to Grandma.

After a while, Grandma called me to the living room and told me Grandma Mittie had passed away, and Mr. Brown had come to get me to be there for her funeral. She told me to pack a couple of changes of clothes because I'd be staying with Mr. Brown a few days. When we got to Mr. Brown's, he explained to me how Grandma Mittie had died. She had a severe asthma attack, and the ambulance couldn't revive her. The day for her funeral came. Mr. Brown and I went. It was at the Jackson Funeral Home, just a couple of blocks from the building on Michigan. There weren't many people there, but I saw my dad. I think Edward was still away at parental school. After the funeral, my dad took me for a walk and said he would come back and take me to spend some time with him at his house. He left, and Mr. Brown took me upstairs. I went into mine and Edward's room. It was an empty feeling and lonely. Grandma was gone now, and I didn't know when or if Edward was ever coming home again. I wasn't sleeping too good in the room. So Mr. Brown had me to come and sleep in his room with him. He had what was called a rollaway bed for me to sleep on. When I'd wake up, he'd have breakfast ready and have my clothes laid out for me. I'd be out of school for about a week. All I had to do was play, eat, and sleep. Mr. Brown didn't watch TV, he only listened to the radio. So I would go into our room and watch TV.

Sometimes, Mr. Brown would still go and visit Edward and would bring back lots of things he had made in woodshop there— shelves, plaques, and lamps made from cow's horns and other jewelry, etc. He also sent pictures of where he lived. The buildings looked like little cottages, and there were farm animals all around; it didn't look like he was locked up at all. It looked more like a place to vacation at or something, but I thought I still wouldn't want to be there so far away from my family, not being able to see them when I want. I'd never end up in a place like that.

After Grandma Mittie's passing, Grandma Joanna felt that I could spend more time with Mr. Brown so she arranged for me to be transferred from my school to a school near Mr. Brown so I could visit with him after school before coming home. I was still able to spend weekends with him. We'd go out to restaurants to eat some- times, but Mr. Brown mostly cooked for himself. He'd take me to the movies and on long train rides to visit with a lady friend of his who lived in sort of a countrylike area where there were barns, cows, horses, and chickens. It was very different than the South Side. I always looked forward to those trips.

Then summer vacation time came. And Grandma agreed to let me spend the whole summer with Mr. Brown. I was having the time of my life. All I had to do every day was get up, go watch a little TV, eat breakfast, and go out and play until dark. Most times, I stayed close to the building and played by myself chasing and catching grasshoppers, butterflies, etc. But on occasions, I'd sneak off and go up on the side of some old train tracks and sit where I could see most of the neighborhood. I just watch the people walking up and down the streets and cars driving by and children playing around the build- ings and in the playgrounds. Sometimes, I'd sit for hours forgetting the time. Then I'd head home and when I got near, I could hear Mr. Brown calling for me. Then I'd see him, and he'd ask where I had been but never scold me and would just say to never go too far where I couldn't hear him call for me.

My brother Edward had come home now, and he had gotten a bicycle and would take me riding sometimes. We would ride over to Prairie where Grandma Joanna lived. Edward would go off riding with his friends, and I would play with my friends. I would see Priscilla playing across the street and wished Grandma would let her go back with me and spend the rest of the summer with me at Mr. Browns. I would ask Grandma from time to time, and she'd say, "Some other time." When I got ready to go back, Priscilla would cry and ask to go with me. I missed her, and she missed me. Edward would come back and get me to take me back to Mr. Brown's, and he'd leave again on his bike. He didn't have a curfew at night. At night, I still stayed in Mr. Brown's room.

Later, Edward began to come home less and less and eventually not at all. I missed him telling me stories about his time in parental school and the bike rides over to Prairie. It was kind of lonesome now even with seemingly having hundreds of toys to play with. It would've been good if Priscilla could come to stay for a while. Then one day, while I was out playing around at the back of the building, I heard a whimpering sound coming out from a grassy area of a vacant lot across the alley way. I went to see what it was. I was always inquisitive and adventurous. When I got over there, I could see something sort of black and white moving in the grass. It was a tiny puppy. I was always told not to be too fast to grab and pick up animals, but this one sounded so helpless, so I found some old newspaper and wrapped it inside and took it upstairs.

When Mr. Brown saw it, he smiled and said, "Oh, you've found a little friend?" He told me how to care for it. It was a boy puppy, so I named him Duke. That name, to me, sounded like it made him important and strong.

I was so happy to have duke. As he grew, he'd begun to follow me up and down the hallway. I really grew attached to him. I didn't want to let him out of my sight. I wanted him to sleep with me, but Mr. Brown said dogs belong on the floor. Duke had a little blanket he slept on, and many times, I'd get down on the floor and sleep with him. I didn't want to take him outside with me because I didn't want anything to happen to him. But Mr. Brown told me that dogs need to get air and be able to run and exercise. So I began to take him out with me but not going from in front of the building. We'd run and play up and down the block. Duke was very smart and easily followed any command I gave him. I never knew what breed of dog he was until one day, when he was older, I learned he was a shepherd collie, mostly used in herding sheep, and that they were among some of the smartest dogs for obedience and intelligence. I was so proud to have him.

One day, Mr. Brown said he needed to buy something from "The Catholic Salvage." I had passed there with him many times and saw people coming and going in and out with different things, but we never went in. I was so happy to finally see what goes on inside that big building. It looked like just a great big church to me. But once inside, *wow*! All the things and people all over the place, this was an adventure for me. Mr. Brown let me walk around and browse on my own. There was so much to look at, but nothing that really caught my undivided attention. Then all of a sudden, I saw something. It was a shiny new bicycle. I found Mr. Brown and showed it to him; he agreed to buy it for me. I could hardly wait to get it home. My brother Edward had taught me how to ride a little on his bike, but it was much too big for me.

I'd ride my bike up and down the sidewalk, up and down the alley way with Duke running right beside me. Now I couldn't wait to show it off to my friends on Prairie after Mr. Brown was confident that I could ride well enough to ride long distance. He walked me to Thirty-Fifth Street and Michigan; there was a traffic light there. And he told me to always cross at the traffic light and stay on the sidewalks. I had Duke tied to my handle bars. I'd go and play with my friends and let some of them have rides until it was time to go back. I'd get Priscilla and ride her for a couple of rides before I left. I so hated to ride off and leave her.

Well, summer had come to an end, and it was time to go home. When Mr. Brown would walk me, I wanted the walk to take a long, long time, and after he had taken me into the house, I'd stand at

Grandma's big picture window and watch him as he crossed the vacant lot until he'd disappear. I wasn't sad but didn't want the summer fun to end. Although I would be able to see and play with Duke every day, I still didn't have all the time I had to run and play with him for hours, and I couldn't take him with me when I'd go back home on Prairie. So each time I saw him, it was as if he hadn't seen me for weeks. He was so happy and frisky each time.

Well, the school season was over once again. Summer vacation had come. I'd be going to spend the summer with Mr. Brown and Duke. I'd gotten big enough now to go by myself. This summer, Grandma surprised me. She let Priscilla go with me to spend a couple of weeks. I took her for rides on my bike, ran, and played with Duke, and we'd play with our toys up and down the hallway. We were having such fun together. We found out that Mom and George had opened a basement candy store across the street on Michigan. Michigan was about a four-lane street—very, very busy. The cars seemed to move as if they were on a racing track. Then one day, while we were out playing, Priscilla wanted candy, so we started out for Mom's candy store. We had Duke with us. I had him on a leash. But as usual, he was very frisky and jumping all about as if he knew we were going somewhere different this time.

On the way down to the corner, Priscilla begged and begged me to let her hold the leash. Priscilla was sort of frail-like, so I told her no because I was afraid that Duke would pull her down and drag her, and I'd be in a lot of trouble. But she begged and begged me. As we got to the corner to cross to the store, I said *okay* and had her to hold the leash tight with both hands. I ordered Duke to sit while we waited for some cars to pass; instead, he bolted into the street pulling Priscilla with him. I shouted for her to let go! For some reason, she couldn't. Then I saw the cars hit Duke and then Priscilla, knocking her up into the air, and it seemed that car after car hit her to no end. Then they suddenly stopped, and there lay my little sister all twisted and bloody; I ran over to her.

My mom came out from hearing the noise of the accident. People were all around; I began to shake all over. Mom came and got me and pulled me onto the sidewalk. People were running from the direction of Prairie Street. I could see some of my cousins and uncles and everybody. How did they know so fast? My mom was crying and crying and asking how did it happen? As I explained to her, I remembered that I didn't see Duke anywhere. The ambulance came and took Priscilla away. Mom had wanted me to come down into the candy store with her, but I had to find Duke. The street was blocked off, so I crossed back over to go to the building. I saw Mr. Brown at the corner. He hugged me with tears in his eyes; he held me and kept saying he was sorry. As we walked back to the building, I told him I couldn't find Duke. He told me Duke had come upstairs.

We went upstairs, and I could see Duke's tail coming from under Mr. Brown's bed. He was whining. I called him; he began to turn around under the bed toward me. I went to pull him out, but Mr. Brown told me to leave him. He said because when animals are wounded like that, it's not good to touch them because they don't know that you're trying to help and they might bite you. As I looked at him, I could see his mouth was broken, and one leg seemed it wasn't attached too good. All I could do was look at him and cry. Mr. Brown told me that he probably wouldn't live through the night. I sat on the floor in front of him most of the night. He closed his eyes and was quiet. I thought he was sleep, so I said my prayers and went to bed. When I awoke the next morning, he wasn't there. I asked Mr. Brown where he was. Mr. Brown said he had died last night, and he took him out to the vacant lot and buried him. He took me out to where he was, and it was almost in the exact same place I found him when he was a puppy. I could only think I've lost my little sister and my dog on the same day and began to feel it was all my fault. Without them, it wouldn't be such a fun summer. I wouldn't be walking Priscilla to school, no more running and playing with Duke and having him run alongside my bicycle when I'd ride over to Prairie. I felt like my little world had ended. I'd go and spend time at Mom's candy store a lot, and Mr. Brown would still take me places, and I'd still ride my bike over to Prairie to play, but nothing was the same; I'd play some and then go off to myself and just sit and think.

Well, summer vacation was coming to a close once again. And it would be back to my usual routine. But before it was completely over, I found out that Grandma was moving, and I could stay with Mr. Brown until she'd send for me. Not long after Grandma got sick and went to the hospital, I thought, maybe, I'd be staying with Mr. Brown for a longer time now. And I'd be able to stay at my school around my friends and be able to see my other friends and family more on Prairie. But it wasn't long before someone was knocking at the door. It was my cousin Marvin. He said Grandma was home from the hospital, and she wanted me to come home. He told me Grandma had moved to Sixty-Third and Greenwood Street. I had no idea where that was, but it sounded as though it was a very long way away. It also seemed like it was cousin Marvin and I walked all the way. When we got there, the apartment was about as big as the one on Prairie. Grandma was all unpacked, and Howard and I had our own beds whereas before, we had shared one bed. My Uncle JW had his room, and Grandma had her room. There was a nice big kitchen and a big living room with a big picture window. The elevated train ran right outside of uncle JW's room window. Cousin Marvin stayed awhile then was leaving. I hated to see him go. I wanted so much to go back with him and I thought, *I'm so far away now. How would Mr. Brown know where to come to get me?* We ate dinner and went to bed. I cried all that night silently, of course, because Grandma didn't stand for a lot of bawling and tantrum-throwing.

The next morning, things looked strange to me in more ways than one. There wasn't a pot-bellied stove in the living room like on Prairie that we had to keep filled with coal to heat the living room. The front bedrooms, and where was the coal stove for the kitchen? I walked back to the hallway; there was no coal bin closet where the coal was kept. How would we warm the house for winter? Grandma explained we had steam heat that comes up from the basement and heats the radiators that we had in just about every room.

Grandma asked my uncle JW to show me where the garbage cans were downstairs so that I could empty the garbage. There was a door that led out to the street; my uncle walked me out, and right next door, there was a barber shop that he owned. He showed me around and then showed me my directions. What was north, south, east, and west because I had no clue. He showed me the train track on Sixty-

21

Third Street where the train would travel from the University Street station, one block over, and travel west and then north to Thirty-Fifth Street and farther. I was good at remembering street names and which streets were next to which. So if I ever wanted to ride or walk anywhere, I would be okay. I wondered if Mr. Brown would know how to find me and if he would come that far to get me.

Well, Grandma got me enrolled in my new school. It was within walking distance from the house, just a couple of blocks or so. I learned the route very quickly, and it was okay; my teachers liked me. I did very well in all my classes and was soon assigned to patrol boy. That was a student-crossing guard. All of this was good, but I still missed the old neighborhood and my friends. Each time I saw the train or bus heading that direction, I longed to, one day, be on one going that way.

Meanwhile, I made a few friends at school; we participated in lots of school projects and activities together. It wasn't long before we were hanging out together getting into mischief. Not too bad of things, just smoking cigarettes, sneaking a little alcohol, and drinking sometimes, skipping classes and playing hooky until school was out. The biggest thing we ever did was to break into school on weekends to steal school supplies from the supply room. Some we'd keep for ourselves and some we'd sell to other students. When I'd take mine home, I would sneak in the house quietly. I had a key and sneak past the living room to my room and stash everything on a shelf above the room door that I thought Grandma never paid any attention to. Howard, sometimes seeing me and not understanding, would sometimes ask aloud what I was doing, so I had to give him candy to not talk about it to Grandma. That didn't last long.

One day, when I came in from school, Grandma was sitting in front of the big picture window as she always did. She said God doesn't like thieves and liars! I knew right then she was talking about me. I dare not lie to her because that would mean certain whipping and punishment. The truth would mean only punishment and her telling everybody that came to the house what I had done, constant shame, and my privileges on hold for who knows how long. So I told her and endured my punishment and shame. She never asked if there was anybody else involved with me. Her focus was always on what her children did or didn't do and not on someone else's children. I wouldn't have told her anyway. Well, goodbye leisure and playtime. And I knew that would include visiting with Mr. Brown. I wondered, *Did he even know our address, or did he even have the phone number? I've done it now*, I thought. *I'd probably never see him again.* Weekends came and went and no Mr. Brown. Every time the phone rang, I was waiting for Grandma to say, "Hello, Mr. Brown." Each time a knock came at the door, I'd run to open it hoping Mr. Brown would be standing there. It never happened. Then one day, someone came and told Grandma that Mr. Brown had passed away a couple of weeks before. I cried and cried and wondered why everything and everyone close to me had to die. Grandma explained to me that death was a part of life, and that's why it's important to do right by people and things you care about because they won't always be there for you.

I hadn't seen my mom since the day Priscilla died. I had wanted to go and see her. But Grandma wouldn't let me travel by myself. And it seemed that no one was ever going that way that could take me with them to see her. I couldn't wait for the day that I could just get up and go as I pleased with no one to tell me when to come and go. But even though I knew how and where to go, how would I get there? I had no money of my own. Grandma would give me money for candy and to buy from the restaurant sometimes and show fare on weekends. So I asked Grandma if I could do chores and errands for some of the neighbors after school and save my money to buy things myself sometimes. She agreed. I felt really good to be earning my own money. Seemed like things were brightening up for me. I came home from school one day, and my mom was there with Grandma. She was lying on the couch. She reached up and hugged me and told me she wasn't feeling well. We talked awhile, then she began to fall asleep. Grandma told me to let her rest. I went and did my homework and my chores, then later went to bed for school the next day.

That next morning, I went to say good morning to my mom; she had gone into Grandma's room. I went in and called to her; she didn't answer. I shook her; she didn't move. Her legs were hanging half off the bed. I told Grandma, and she said Mom was tired and for me to leave her alone, and I'd see her after school. I had my breakfast and went off to school. I couldn't wait until school was out to get home and talk with Mom.

When I got in, Grandma was in the kitchen cooking. She had made Mom some soup and asked me to take it to her. I did. Mom was sitting on the side of the bed. As she ate, we talked awhile about her and George, times at the restaurant, Georgette's death, and when Priscilla had died. She explained a lot to me that day, most I understood but some I didn't. We talked about how I was doing in school and how she wanted Howard and me to come and visit with her. She told me that her and George had gotten another restaurant, and they were doing a lot better. She said she'd talk to Grandma about her coming to get us one day. I asked her why we couldn't come to live with her. She said she'd explain that at another time. We laughed and talked awhile more, then Mom said she wanted to rest. I left and went to my room.

The next morning, when I awoke, I got dressed for school and was going in to say goodbye to Mom. Grandma told me to let her rest, and she'd be here when I got home. After school, I ran home as fast as I could; my first stop once in the house was Grandma's room. I went in, and Mom was gone. Grandma said she had felt much better and had to get back to the restaurant. Mom had left me a few dollars with Grandma and told her to tell me she loved us, Howard and I, and she'd be back soon to see us. I asked Grandma if one of my uncles could take me to see her. But I was reminded that I was still on punishment. Seemed like it had been forever already.

Now I was really anxious to get away just for a little while to be able to go back to the old neighborhood and see my old friends. But I couldn't see any of the family, or they would get word to Grandma, and I'd really be in for it then. I decided it would work if I went to school a couple of days straight and missed one and went the next couple of days and write a note each time with a different excuse and sign Grandma's name to it. Grandma wouldn't know the difference as long as I was home at the same time each day. If I were a few minutes late getting back, I always had a good excuse for her. So I'd skip a couple of classes from time to time and take the train to Thirty-Fifth Street, hang out with my friends, get into all kinds of mischief including smoking and drinking a little alcohol that older guys would buy for us and sometimes stealing from neighborhood stores. I was always careful to stay off the streets where I might run into a relative. I would always leave in time to take the Cottage Grove Street bus back to Sixty-Third because it was the closet to Greenwood for me to get back home at the right time as if I had been to school. My older sister Maryann and my cousin Cathryn shared an apartment on Sixty-Second and Calumet. Sometimes, I would walk to their place and spend the day. They'd let me stay there. I'd watch TV, eat junk food, and play games. But they'd always encourage me to stop ditching school and hanging out on Thirty-Fifth Street, but it went in one ear and out the other. Soon, my skipping school caught up with me.

Grandma found out about everything I had been doing. She gave me a whipping I wasn't soon to forget. My restrictions became harder and harder, and my chores were doubled. I resented every second of it—knowing that it was my fault but feeling I didn't deserve as harsh a punishment. I got to the point where I stopped crying when I got a whipping. A deep anger built up in me that I had to suppress. By now, I was twelve, and all I could think of is that I couldn't wait for the chance to run away and never come back. I felt that when I turn thirteen, then I could leave, and I would be old enough that Grandma wouldn't send anybody to look for me. I don't know why I thought that, but that was my mindset, and I had to make it happen.

Grandma was never mean to me; it was just that I felt ready to live my own life. I had no idea where I would go or where I would live or how I would survive; I just wanted out. Then one day, while I was taking the garbage out, I heard someone calling out watermelons like the guys would do when they came by on the horse and wagon selling. I peeked out of the door to the street. It was my brother James and a couple of other workers. I waved and called out to him. He called to me to come over to the wagon. I thought, *This is it. I'll get away with my brother*. He wouldn't mind taking me as he and Grandma weren't on such good terms anyway. When I got to the wagon, I started to climb on. But James told me to get down. I told him how I had been feeling and how I wanted to get away back to the old neighborhood to my friends and how I'd like to live with him. He gave me a watermelon to take upstairs to Grandma and told me he would come back to get me next time. Days and weeks passed; other wagons would pass but no James. Well, I thought, *I guess he didn't want to be anymore at odds with Grandma than he already was.* I went about my regular routines without showing any displeasure and causing any reason for more punishment.

Then one day, as I was emptying the garbage, I heard the sound of hoof clacking down the street. I peeked out, and it was my brother James. As he parked the wagon across the street, he waved for me to come over. When I got across the street, he had one of the other guys take a watermelon to Grandma, and he told me to meet him around the corner. I bent down and crept alongside the parked cars to the corner and around hoping Grandma wasn't sitting at the window and see me once around the corner. I climbed up into the wagon, and James told me to get under the seat and told the other guys to put straw all in front of me. He told me to stay there until he said to come out. I felt relieved I was finally getting away.

After a while, James said I could get up. I sat on the wagon seat next to him. He let me hold the reins to the horse and was teaching me how to guide it, to stop it, and make it go. He also taught me how to call out for selling the watermelons. On the routes, as he called out, people would stop in their cars to buy or call from their windows up to three and four floors high. The people asked to pick out the watermelon they asked for. Sometimes, they would ask to see if it was red or ripe. The guys would take a butcher knife from a slot in the wagon seat and cut a triangular shape in it and stick the knife in the middle of it then take it out and hold it up to the customer to see; they would then take it to them. As it was getting late, James would stop the wagon at a chicken restaurant and buy everyone an order then stop at a grocery store and buy two to three large bottles of soda. He sent one guy to the liquor store to buy some wine. After eating, James pulled the wagon under the elevated train tracks, and they started drinking wine and smoking cigarettes; I asked to participate, but James wouldn't let me. That was okay. One day, I'd be able to do it too with no one to tell me I can't. It was night now, and James came across Thirty-Fifth Street and pulled into an alley between Giles and Prairie Streets. I asked where we were going and he said to the barn. I had been across Thirty-Fifth Street many times, but I didn't know there was a horse barn there. In the alley, James had me to get down off the wagon as he drove the horse inside a big wide wooden gate. As I looked in, I could see a few stacks of watermelons on the ground and a couple of wagons. As I stood there, more wagons came and went into the big yard.

Everybody got down off their wagons, unhitched the horses, and led them out of the gate to a barn next door. When James had put his horse away, he took me to his house where he lived with a woman named Betty. When we came in, James introduced me as his little brother and told Betty that I would be staying with them for a while. For the first few weeks, everything was going good. It seemed that Betty didn't mind me staying there. She and James had a baby girl. Her name we Deidra. She was my niece. I would babysit her when James and Betty would go out for the evening. And I did errands for Betty when she asked. I thought I was doing good until one night, I overheard them arguing; Betty was saying how I wasn't doing any chores like laundry, sweeping, mopping, etc., but I was eating up a lot of food and just staying out 'til late and getting up and going to the watermelon yard with James every day, and she didn't like it. James would argue back, and they went back and forth. This started to happen a lot. I began to feel I was the cause of it and that it would be better if I left. But where would I go? And what would I do?

I made my mind up that I'd leave. So I did. There was no Mr. Brown to go to. I didn't know where my dad was, so I went to Mom's candy store, but it was closed and padlocked; now, what would I do? I discovered that my dad's old car was still in back of the building where Grandma Mittie and Mr. Brown had lived. So it was somewhere to sleep at least. I was scared every minute of sounds during the night, and the nights were cold with nothing but my jacket to cover up with. What would I do for food and clothes? I knew I couldn't live like this for long. I did it for a couple of days and nights, just wandering around trying to stay out of the way of the truant officers and police that Grandma Joanna might have looking for me.

One day, I went to Prairie Street to see some of my friends; we played baseball, football, and other games. As it got later, everyone started to thin out and go in for the night. I thought to myself it was back to the abandoned car on Michigan again. But I saw my friend David and told him my story, and he said there was a way I could stay with him and I could share his clothes and to not worry about eating. He lived with his dad who worked nights and came home around 7:00 a.m. So I stayed with David quite a while doing that arrangement, although I had to be out by 7:00 a.m. until 11:00 p.m. or so. But during the day, David hung out with me. He didn't go to school either, but it was okay with his dad. We'd spend time at some other girls' house where they went to school when they pleased, and their mom didn't mind us coming over and staying as long as we wanted. The mom had a drinking problem and stayed inebriated most of the time.

Then one day, I saw my brother James coming out of the alley on his horse and wagon, and he asked why I left and where was I staying. I told him my story, and he told me I could come back and stay with him and Betty again and that she was sorry that I had left. I agreed, and James had me to ride his wagon with him. From that point, everything seemed to be looking up. I felt good working everyday with my brother and him paying me a few dollars at the end of the week. Before long, the other watermelon guys saw how I worked with James, and they wanted me to work with them. James told them that they would have to pay me $125 a week, and he didn't want them overworking me like he'd seen them do some other young boys. Eventually, I did work for one of the other guys, and later, my cousin David came to work at the yard. It wasn't long before he was given his own horse to drive. I had always wanted to drive my own horse, but I was short and not too stocky and didn't seem that I could handle it. I could, but I was content with what I was doing so far.

David's family had moved from Prairie to Wabash. So one night, after work, David asked me to come and spend the night with him. I was reluctant because his mom, Aunt Ida Mae, was Grandma's daughter. And I knew she would call and tell Grandma I was there. But David knew when his mom and dad would be turning in for the night, and he'd sneak me in, and we'd be leaving out before they awoke. It worked, so I began staying at David's. I told my brother James, and he was glad because David and I had grown up to be more like brothers than cousins and had always stood by one another no matter what and no matter the odds.

David had become a member of the Del Viking street gang around the neighborhood and introduced me to it. State Street was our main street, but the areas we controlled went from State Street at Thirty-Fifth to Thirty-Ninth and east to south parkway; there were other neighborhoods further south, east, and west where other gangs merged with us. There was always a few gang fights off and on when someone would enter someone else's neighborhood for a party or something. Those were mainly physical confrontations. There were very few guns, and they were seldom used. And one thing the gang demanded was respect for elders and anyone that lived in the neighborhood. We didn't tolerate robberies, burglaries, and definitely no rapes in our neighborhoods. I'd hang out from time to time on weekends on some days when the watermelon guy I worked with didn't show up; Saturday was payday at the watermelon yard. On Saturdays, some of us would meet up on Indiana Street and race our wagons to the barn at Thirty-Fifth. The wagons would sway back and forth, and sometimes the leftover watermelons would fall off and burst all over the street. That was really a fun time for me.

After being paid Saturday night, on Sunday morning we went off to Twelfth Street to what we called Jew Town because mostly, all the businesses there were owned by Jews. We always went there to shop for clothes, jewelry, and other good deals. I'm now having the time of my life. Then one day, while we're having fun on State Street, someone decided that we should go and steal some bicycles from some white boys. Four or five of us went down State Street to Twenty-Second and snatched some bicycles. The police was called, and we rode off on the bikes toward Thirty-Fifth Street, zigzagging through alleys and vacant lots. Before I knew it, a police car was on me. They caught me and took me to the police station. They asked who they could call to come and talk to them because if no one came, they would take me to the Audy Home on Roosevelt Road where runaways and truants were sent. I had heard about it but never wanted to go there. I only knew one phone number they could call. That was Grandma.

They called and said someone would be there to pick me up. Hours passed, and I really wanted to leave that police station, but all I could think of was my freedom is over, and all the good times are gone, and I'd probably get the whipping of my life and never get off punishment. And there was no sense trying to get away again. And if I did since the police had caught me, there would be a very slim chance of staying with my brother James or with David again. Well, I had brought it on myself all for a bicycle. Why? Just to be cool with the guys or just being a follower? I had a good job working the watermelon wagon and had my own money and freedom to spend it when and however I wanted. I could have bought my own bike.

My uncle JW came and picked me up. I got a full verbal chastisement all the way from the police station to home after he got through. It was like I'd been whipped already. When we got to the house, I braced for what was to come next. When we came in, Grandma was sitting at the window with her back turned. She told uncle JW that she was tired and angry and if she whipped me, she was afraid what she'd do to me. So she told him to do it. My uncle took me into the bathroom. He told me that he really did understand what I felt and wanted to do, but it was very hard and painful on Grandma, and the older I got, the harder it was going to be for me in the streets. He said he wasn't going to whip me because he could see it wouldn't do any good at this point. So he told me he was going to be hitting the bathtub and the shower curtain, and he wanted me to cry and plead like he was whipping me good. When he was finished, he told me to go down the hallway, sniffling and moaning.

Grandma reinstated me in school and had uncle JW to walk with me to the corner of the school building and watch to make sure I went in. Then after school, he'd be at the corner to walk me to the house. A couple of months or so passed, then I figured out how I could get away without uncle JW seeing me. I remembered that at the end of the day, the janitor always used the rear door for taking trash out to the alley. From there, I could go over to University Street without uncle JW seeing me, and I could make it to the train to Thirty-Fifth Street. I took the train. And as I passed our building, I said to myself I'd never have to see it again. Somehow, I understood that Grandma was only trying to do good for me. But it wasn't what I wanted and that I had to do this and I'd prove I didn't make a bad decision. Now all I had to do was be smart about it and make it until I'd be sixteen, four years to go, then I didn't have to dodge and hide from the truant officers and police.

When I got to Thirty-Fifth, it was still school hours, so I walked around staying off of the main streets until 3:15 p.m. when school was out. Had I gotten there earlier, maybe I could've gone out on one of the watermelon wagons. The police never bothered to check how old the boys were who worked on the wagons. All my friends were glad to see me. We hung out all that day. But when it began to get dark, they began to go in. Now what would I do? Where would I sleep? It was close to 10:00 p.m. I went around the alley toward the watermelon yard; the gate was locked. I was hoping to see my brother James and see if he would let me stay with him again. Then I heard the clapping of horse hooves. I was praying it was James. It wasn't him. It was Michael, the younger brother of the owner, Rodger who ran the watermelon barnyard along with his mother, Ms. Annette, and his uncle who was called Bean. Anyway, after Michael took care of his wagon and the horse, he was about to lock up the yard when I told him I had nowhere to stay that night. He let me spend the night in the yard but said I had to leave before opening time at 8:00 a.m. So about 7:00 a.m., I climbed the fence and sat across the alley to wait for the guys to show up for work and see who I could ride with that morning. When they did, my brother James had gotten his helpers already and so had my cousin David, and it seemed so had everyone else.

There was one more wagon pulling out. It was one of the guys everyone called Gunslinger. I guess he was called that because he always dressed western style and sort of dressed his horse up something like you'd see in cowboy movies. He asked me if I want to work;

31

I said yes, so I got on. There was another boy we called Lips because of his large prominent lips. He didn't mind being called that, but all the other guys always taunted and made fun of him and many times took advantage of him. He and I became friends. We'd all always have breakfast at a restaurant called Callie's Kitchen. No one would ever sit with him. And he hardly ever had money enough to pay for breakfast. I had friends who would loan me until payday, so I would always help him out. Actually, the guys at the yard were sort of like one big family. Anyone outside of our group caused problems with anyone of us, we were all there for them. That went for Lips too no matter how they rode him from time to time.

Well, when we came back to the yard that night, I thought I could maybe go home with my brother James or David. I didn't want to spend another night in the watermelon yard. But when brother James's wagon came in, he wasn't on it. So I waited for David's wagon to come in. When he got settled, we went to the "Tasty Freeze" ice cream store at the corner of the alley. He asked where I'd been staying. I told him, and he said to come with him. I wondered if he was taking me to Aunt Ida Mae's. I didn't think that would go well. But when we got to his building, he told me about some of the guys in the gang hanging out in the laundry room of one of the projects the Stateway Gardens on State Street where we hung out all the time and that they always hung out there and would spend the night with their girlfriends there. I knew all the guys, so I felt right at home; it was somewhere to stay and lots of good company. I met a girl named Valmea; we liked each other, and she would come and spend nights with me there. We always had to be out of there before the tenants would come to wash early the next morning. But one night, when I went to the laundry room, it was locked. It hadn't been locked before. So here I was back where I started. I slept in the stairwell that night.

The next day, I went to work at the watermelon yard. That night, David sneaked me in again. The next morning, I found out my cousin Bernice, his older sister, had moved across the hall from their mom. So David took me over to ask her if I could stay there. She agreed. So I stayed with Bernice and her children. It was a long time before Aunt Ida Mae know I was staying with Bernice. Even when she later found out, she didn't make a big deal out of it. I continued to work on the watermelon wagons. David and I bought watermelons home to Aunt Ida Mae and Bernice every night, and we'd bring ice cream, candy, and goodies home for his sisters and brothers, niece, and nephews. As I continued to work the wagons, I hadn't seen my brother James for a while. I asked where he was, and I was told he had "gone south." I thought he had moved further south or something. Then I learned when it's said that one of the guys went south, it meant they had run off with the watermelon money. But that they'd come back next year. They'd mostly do this close to the close of the season.

Anyway, one payday, most of the guys were going to the hair-style shop for men on Forty-Seventh Street—a shop called Jessie's. Most of the guys already had processed hair and hair straightened with lye cream. They were getting theirs redone and some for the first time. That payday, David and I got our hair done. It made a big difference in my attitude. I really felt grown up now, and who could tell me anything? The girls were flirting and wanting to feel my hair. This was the life. Later, I learned that Mom and George had opened a restaurant on Sixty-First and State Street. But I was so caught up in my own new world that it was a couple of months before I got by there, and when I did, it was closed up. I had a chance to see my mom for the first time since she left Grandma's, and I blew it. Now how would I find her? No one else knew where she'd gone.

Then one day, I was standing on the corner of Thirty-Fifth and Giles, and I saw somebody come by with a snowball cone. I asked where they had gotten it, and they said from a truck on Prairie Street. So I walked down there, and lo and behold, it was George and Mom selling like they used to. I ran up and hugged her. George spoke, and he seemed to have a different attitude. Mom and I talked for a long while. I told her I had left Grandma's and wasn't going back. She told me that her and George had moved to Thirty-Eight and South park that was just four blocks east of Prairie and three blocks south. They both said I was welcome to come and stay with them anytime. I was so happy to hear that. This was the best of everything that could happen for me. By this time, I was only thirteen and had lived like a vagabond for well over a year but to no one's fault but my own. But this was it. I wasn't going to blow this no matter what.

Mom gave me a key and told me I could come and go as I pleased but just try and stay out of trouble. I did. For the next few months, everything was going so good until one night, after work at the watermelon yard, Lips came to me with a crazy idea. I don't know why I ever agreed to it. Maybe because I felt exceptionally good and because I had a little alcohol in me from drinking with the older guys as they would sometimes allow us to do. Lips wanted me to go with him to Forty-third Street where a guy had a garage where he kept Shetland ponies that he used to sell rides to children in Washington Park on weekends. We were going to break in and steal them for a joyride and bring them back. It was 1:00 a.m., and we were clippety-clopping up and down the streets. Finally, we went through one alley, and the police was right behind us. We jumped off the ponies and run. The police caught up to us and held us while waiting for the owner to come. Then I saw my chance; I broke away and ran down the alley toward the street. One of the officers chased behind me. When I got to the street, there was a parked car. I quickly slid under it. It wasn't parked far from a corner; when the officer got to the street, he stopped a moment and looked around a bit then walked to the corner and back up the street. He couldn't see me under the car; it was too dark. I could hear their car pull up. The officer that chased me said, "He had gotten away." He didn't know how I could disappear so fast. Then I heard them laugh and say, "At least, we caught one of them." My heart was racing, and I was doing my best not to cough; my asthma had flared up, and I was wheezing and as scared as I could be. Then I heard them drive off. I waited for what seemed like another hour, then I crawled from under the car and walked to south park crouching down behind parked cars all the way home.

Mom and George were asleep when I came in. I didn't sleep so well that night. I was worrying if Lips had told on me and the police would come knocking at the door. Nothing happened. So the next morning when I got up, Mom was already up fixing breakfast. I hugged her and said goodbye and that I'd see her later that night. Well, that didn't happen because when I got almost to the yard, a police detective car stopped me and asked my name. I told him, and he said that Lips had told the arresting officers from that night my name and that I worked at the watermelon yard; he had described me to them. I denied it. But when I got to the station, the arresting officer who I'd run from that night was there and identified me. I gave them my mom's number this time hoping she would come and get me. But there was no answer; She and George must have been out in the truck. And if I didn't come in that night, Mom would just figure I had maybe spent the night at David's or Bernice's. No one would know where I was since no one I knew saw them put me in the car. And Lips probably wouldn't go back to the yard and tell what happened since he told on me. So the only thing left to do was for them to call Grandma. When they called Grandma, I heard them tell her that, that was my second arrest for theft, and they would be sending me to the Audy Home on Roosevelt Road. Also, that I would have to go to court, and she could get all the information there.

I sat at the station all that morning until later that evening when a bus came and took me away. There were other boys already on the bus when I got in. It wasn't long before we arrived at the Audy Home; when we arrived, we were issued uniforms to put on. Our street clothes were bagged, labeled, and taken away. Our uniforms had numbers and a letter on them. We were split up into groups. I guess the numbers and letters identified us and what area we were going to because we all went different ways down different hallways. We were given sheets pillows and blankets, face towels, bath towels, toothbrush, toothpaste, and slippers.

Then we were directed to some rooms. There were two beds in each room and two small bedside tables with a drawer and a bottom shelf. Once we were settled, we were called out in the hall to stand by our room door, and a guard came down the line counting us. When he was done, we were taken to the bathroom to wash our hands, and then we were taken to a large room with lots of tables and chairs. Other groups of boys that weren't on the bus with us also came in. Once we all were seated, someone came in with a food cart full of trays of sandwiches and juices. We were told we had missed dinner. We had fifteen minutes to eat, and then it would be time to go to bed. Lights out, total darkness in the room. The only light is the dim light from the hall in front of your door. Doors weren't locked at night so you could go to the toilet. The day room was locked at night. And there was a guard at the end of the hall.

The next morning, we woke up around 7:00 a.m.; we went in to shower and dress to go into the day room. Then about 9:00 a.m., breakfast would come. That morning, more boys came to the day room. I knew a few of them from State Street—my friends from the gang. All had been pretty peaceful until then. Some of my friends started fights and other problems. There was a rule that when you get into trouble too many times, you'd be sent to "the hole." The hole was a dark room, smaller than the sleeping room. It had one small screened window that faced the hallway. You were given blankets and a pillow, but you slept on the floor. It wasn't cold but very uncomfortable. You'd stay there from 1 day to a week depending on how many times you caused trouble and what the trouble was. During that time, you couldn't have visitors. I ended up in the hole a few times from joining in with my friends. Because it couldn't get out that I didn't help when there was trouble. Well, I ended up in the hole a few times too many. Not for defending myself but defending my friends who instigated the trouble. I had to stand up for myself and let them know I'm looking forward to getting out of here soon and didn't want to spend more time in the hole and keep losing my visits.

The Audy Home normally kept boys about two months unless they were extremely problematic. When your court date was coming up, you were told, and your relatives were told to bring you a change of clothes to wear. Going to court didn't necessarily mean you would be going home. Many times, some went to court and came right back to stay longer or wait to be sent to another institution.

By the time my court date came up, I hadn't been in anymore trouble as most of those friends of mine had either gone home or had been sent to other institutions. Well, the guard brought me my change of clothes, and I was more than ready to go home or just get out of there. I said goodbye to everybody. They all wished me good luck. I was so glad to see Grandma there. She had a very stern face and didn't smile at me. I told her I would obey her and be good from now on. She started to say something, but just then, we were called into the courtroom. It would be over soon, and I'd be on my way home, finally. But when the judge called Grandma and I up, the court officer began to read off all the times I had been truant and had run away from home. And the times I had been caught by the police for stealing. Then the judge said to Grandma that given my record, it shows that she cannot be sure that I wouldn't repeat the things I had done and worse. And that, in her opinion, I need time to think about all the trouble and pain I've caused her.

Grandma said, "Well, maybe you're right. I hate to send him away, but maybe it's best." This was the one time I cried like a baby and begged Grandma to take me home with her. She cried too and said, "I did all I could do." Now it's up to God! She left the courtroom. When they brought me out, my uncle JW was in the hallway; he hugged me and said, "It'll be alright, and it shouldn't be long. Then the guard came out and handed Grandma some papers. Then the guard took me back to the unit. When I got back, I was told to stay dressed in my street clothes. Later that afternoon, some more guys who had gone to court also came back to the unit in their street clothes and waited. Later, our names were called to line up in the hallway. I didn't reminisce too much on the times I had my freedom and lost it or on the days that I wondered how I could get over the walls in the yard. At that moment, I wondered where I was going and for how long. Then I saw a guard come in to the desk down the hall. He gave the guard a list and said these are for "parental." I thought maybe that meant parent. That maybe, the judge changed her mind and was sending our group home to our parents. I asked one of the guys, and they told me it meant "parental school" where they send you for not going to school, running away from home, and stealing, etc. and that it was way out in the country so that you couldn't escape from there. He said he had been there before, and it wasn't so bad.

After a while, the guard came and filed us down the hall to a red door where a bus was waiting. It didn't click at first, but then it came to me parental is where Edward was before. Later that evening, we arrived at a large building. When we went in, there were offices. Then we were taken upstairs where there were large rooms with about ten or so bunk beds around the walls with some sort of storage boxes at each end. We were told those were to store our personal items that we had brought with us. We chose our own beds. We were given labels with our names on them to put on the storage boxes. Later, someone came to get us for dinner. We entered a large dining room where our plates were already prepared on the tables. After dinner, we went back to our room for bed. I went to the window and peered out into like a big courtyard. There were street lamps on both sides and other buildings like ours and grass and benches in between. It was nothing like the yard at the Audy Home with all concrete and seemed like ten-foot high walls all around. I couldn't wait 'til morning to be able to get out there and walk around.

Then morning came; two people came to wake us up. I asked if we were going out into the yard. I was told that that area was for the staff. And that the bus would be here for us soon. We were brought sandwiches and juice to take with us. The bus came; we were loaded on and on our way. The scenery looked far different than places on the south side. It wasn't long before we were pulling into a large parking lot. There were other buses already there. When we came down off the bus, there were groups of men and women waiting as if they were there to greet us. We all lined up outside the bus. There were like small houses all around inside the fence. When our names were called, they called out A-cottage, B-cottage and C-cottage, etc. Then a man and woman would step forward and take us to one of the small houses (cottage). I was going to G-cottage along with a few of the other boys. The man and woman who were taking us to our cottage were Mr. and Mrs. Donnahue as I recall.

When we got inside, there was a large room set up just like a regular living room. Couches, upholstered armchairs, bookshelves, game tables, television pictures around the walls, and all. It had an atmosphere of home. But not that I could get used to living there. Then there were a few other doors around the room—wooden doors with glass windows in them. We were divided into pairs and shown to rooms. In them were a sitting table, two chairs, a folding cot for each of us, two small dressers, and a mirror; there was one window that faced other cottages. There was a large window in the outer room that faced the grounds that had grass and trees all around. After we were all settled in, we were called to the other room for orientation. We were given the rules of dos and don'ts—an explanation of how things were ran in the compound. We received our schedule of chores in the cottage and other chores on the grounds. And we were shown the layout of the grounds and where educational classes were held. There was also a crafts shop where we could make things of all kinds to send home to our families. We weren't allowed to have any money in our possession. All money was collected and written down in a ledger. The same for when our families brought us money. It was written down in the ledger, and we were given printed paper bucks to trade for things we wanted to buy from "the store"—a place in the compound where we could shop once a week. It carried a variety of items. We were allowed to keep three changes of clothes in our rooms. We had to wash and iron ourselves. Our family was allowed to bring us one set of clothes per week, and we had to send one change back home with them.

It was explained to us that the time we would normally spend there would be six months. But that the cottage parents could recommend that someone be released after four months if they were well-behaved. That would be me. I wanted out of there as soon as possible. Mr. Donnahue also told us that if anyone was thinking about running away from there, they wouldn't stop you, and they'd even fix you a "road sandwich." He said some did get away but were always caught, and they had time added on to their six months. I didn't want to run away. I had been running enough and ended up in here. I wanted to not have to run again after this.

I went to school and did my chores well. There were cows and a pig farm. I even helped out slopping the hogs. I'd never seen live pigs and hogs. The hogs were huge, and we were told they were dangerous. If you tried to climb over the fence near the piglets, they would charge you. There was one guy who tended to them, and he had a special technique for working with them inside the fence. It was a fun experience. On certain days, after school, we were allowed so much time in arts and crafts where we could make anything we wanted. I was really good at making lamps from cow's horns. It was a project that could easily take a whole week to complete. The cutting, shaping, sanding, and the wiring. I stayed busy enough that I didn't think so much about being there. And my visits from my mom and uncle JW were happy ones.

Grandma never came but always sent her love and a letter. Everyone always sent their love. When my clothes came on visitor's day, they were sometimes brand new. Nobody took advantage of anybody. We all got along really well until, one day, a boy named Foley came; I could see he was going to be trouble. He came in bullying and throwing around attitude. He probably had been this route before. I was right; Mr. Donnahue welcomed him back and told him his next visit would be to St. Charles Reform School.

Foley must've sensed that I wasn't scared or thought much of him. He asked where I was from. I told him, and he had heard of the gang and neighborhood. He was from the west side of Chicago and a known tough area too. We became friends, but I didn't go in for the bullying stuff. And he steered clear of the friends I had made. I couldn't be peacekeeper for everybody, and I minded my own business. If there were small insignificant altercations, Mr. and Mrs. Donnahue would talk to the boys and try and settle it peaceably between them. Sometimes when it didn't work, you were punished by having to sit in your room while activities were going on—no movies, arts, and crafts, etc. There was never any physical punishment.

But soon, Mr. and Mrs. Donnahue retired. And then a Mr. Jones became our cottage parent. He wasn't married. He was a short black sort of stocky man and smoked a cigar. The cottage parents were allowed to smoke in a designated lounge-like room. I could tell by his walk and demeanor he was going to be tough on us. His first introduction was, "My name is Mr. Jones. I'm not here to babysit you all but to make you grow up." He said he only asks or tells anyone to do something once. After that, it's you and him. *I wouldn't have any problem*, I thought. Now I only had about four months to go with no problems yet. But that was short-lived.

A new boy came in. His name was Hosea Rodriguez. I couldn't forget him. He and Foley stayed into it with each other and bullied the others. Mr. Jones's way of punishment was nothing like Mr. and Mrs. Donnahue's way. He'd make you go into the shower, wet yourself up, and he would come in and whip you with a leather strap, never on your back just your butt. He dared you to move until he was through. If you did, he'd make you stay there, and he'd come back and start in again.

You could hear the sound of the strap and the hollering and crying even from tough old Foley and Hosea. I had never been whipped like that, and I didn't want to start. One day, Hosea decided to try me for no reason. I was in the kitchen washing dishes when he came in with his plate and didn't scrape it like he should. Food was still on it. He threw it in the dishwater splashing water all over me. I was really angry, but I didn't want trouble. Just then, he began to poke me and started saying the mama jokes. I couldn't take much more. So I grabbed him and pushed him against the sink. I went to punch him, and he moved, and I hit the sink. I felt like I had broken my hand; it hurt so bad. He ran to Mr. Jones and told him I had started a fight with him.

Mr. Jones came and grabbed me. I told him what had happened and that Hosea had instigated it. He said no matter, I was the one who tried to start a fight. He never once asked to look at my hand. He just told me to hit the shower and wait for him. I could barely raise my arm to get undressed. Mr. Jones came into the shower, belt in hand. I held up my hand to him to show him that it was swollen. He came down on it with the belt and said that's what fighting gets you. I cried out in pain. He told me to hold my hands up on the shower wall. I could barely get it partway. He whipped me and kept saying, "Raise your hand up." I tried and tried. I just couldn't, so I just sat down and cowered in the corner of the shower. After that, he told me to dry off and get dressed. I thought that was the end of it. Well, at least he took me to the lounge room and wrapped my hand. He wrapped it so tight until it was cutting my circulation off. I mentioned it to him. But he just said that was good for the swelling to go down faster. I thought maybe I could stay in the room for a few days at least until my hand got well. But I was expected to continue my chores, go to my classes, and do anything else he expected of me.

Along with this, my privileges were suspended—no games, no television, and no after-school arts and crafts. He had the authority to and did suspend two weeks of visits.

Our mail was censored before going out so the family wouldn't know and neither would the administration. It was doubtful; it would've done any good to try and tell any of the teachers or other cottage parents. I feared if I said anything, it would make it worse. I endured, and everything went back to normal. For some reason, Hosea's family hadn't been coming to see him as much, and he began not to have money to trade in for things. So I would share my parental bucks with him, although we had had that confrontation. I felt sorry for him. And that seemed to tone him down quite a bit, and we became good friends. Foley was being transferred to another cottage. And Mr. Jones was leaving the school. We never knew why. We did get some new cottage parents. I don't recall their names, but they were a young couple. I had about three more months to go, and now maybe, I could finish in peace and just go home.

To my surprise, after my fourth month, I was told I'd be going home the next month. Time couldn't pass fast enough for me. I made myself a calendar and paste it on the wall in my room. I would mark the days off one by one. The new cottage parents had started a new tradition at G-cottage. The day before anyone was going home, there would be a special dinner and gifts given. You got to stay up later than usual, and if it was a school week, there was no school for you. Finally, my time had come. Everyone wished me good luck. My uncle JW came to get me. This was the first time I had seen the inside of the main building where the administrators were. We went to the main office where I was signed out, and I hadn't expected it, but they returned the balance of the money I hadn't used from the parental bucks; I thought they just kept what was left.

When Uncle JW got outside, he gave the money to me. I forget how much it was, but it felt good to be free and have some money in my pocket again. We took about two buses before we got to the train toward home. On the way, we talked about things I had gone through before I was put in parental. And what lesson I had learned while in there and what I wanted to do now that I was out. There wasn't any sermons or lectures from Uncle JW; actually, we laughed about a lot of it. As we approached downtown Chicago, he said Grandma had said to him just to come and get me. And whatever I decided to do from there, it was up to me, and I could come home when I wanted to. I thought to myself, *This is it*. I made it. Although I was only about to turn fifteen.

When we got to Thirty-Fifth Street, I told Uncle JW I was going to get off there, and I'd be home later. I guess Grandma was tired and decided to let me learn life on my own. It wouldn't be long before I would be on my own anyway. So I got off the train at Thirty-Fifth Street and walked across to look for some of my friends. I met some here and there along the way, but I was mostly looking for Bobo, Fred, Dwight, and Arthur. As we were really close friends during the times around the watermelon yard. I met up with them, and we had an older guy go into the liquor store and buy us some wine. We went to the alley and talked of old times and about my time in parental. We drank and talked for a few hours, then we started to split up and go our separate ways. The guys were sixteen and a little older. They wouldn't have too much of a problem with their parents about drinking, if at all. Well, I chewed lots of gum and drank pops to try and disguise the smell. I didn't know how Grandma would act.

When I got home, I was reluctant and scared. But to my surprise, it didn't go that bad. I went in and sat with Grandma. I apologized for everything I had done. Then she said to me, "You reap what you sow. And I've decided to let go and let *God*! You'll always have a home as long as I live." I stayed in the room with Howard that night.

The next morning, I went downstairs to Uncle JW's barbershop. I sat around and listened to the older guys telling stories of how they grew up and the hardships they faced when they had responsibilities to deal with. But how the things they went through made them a better man. Then I realized that just wanting to be a man and still doing childish things wasn't the answer. So I asked my Uncle JW where I could get a job. He said I would have to be sixteen to be able to legally work.

It was winter now, and the watermelons were out of season, and the yard was closed down until spring. All I was doing day in day out was going to Thirty-Fifth hanging out. And by now, most of my friends had some kind of jobs. And sometimes, I'd only see them in the evening, and even then, it wasn't like it was because they had to get in early and get their rest for work the next day. I was getting tired of just hanging out and needed something else to do. It almost felt like the world had moved on without me. I went over to State Street. My cousin David and his best friend Charles had been arrested and sent to St. Charles Reformatory. Whenever I had gone to State Street, it was mainly to hang out with my cousin. Now, even that had changed. I went back home, and that night, I lay awake wondering if I could have done things different so that things would be different now.

The next morning, there was a knock at the door. It was Mom. I hugged her so tight and long. I was so happy. Grandma was happy too. Mom said she needed to stay for a while because she had not been feeling well and had been on her feet a lot and hadn't been resting good. And she was really tired and worn out from all the cooking and selling she was doing with George. I left out and let her and Grandma talk. I went downstairs and just sat in front of the building thanking God that it felt like everything was just coming together for me. When I got back upstairs, Grandma was sitting in front of the window humming to herself. She did that sometimes when she was pleased about something. Her bedroom door was slightly ajar and she said to me, "Your mother is resting. Let her sleep." So I went to my room and watched TV with Howard until late, then I went to bed.

The next morning, when I woke up, I went into the living room to see Mom, and she was sitting up on the side of the bed. I asked her how she was doing, and she said she wasn't feeling well. Just then, Grandma called for me to come and get some soup for her. I brought the soup to her. She took a couple of spoonfuls and then lay back down. I told her I'd see her later. I decided to take a ride down to Thirty-Fifth Street and hang out for a while. This was the weekend, so the guys would be hanging out late. That night, I got in late. I said good night to Grandma and went to bed.

The next morning, there was a knock at the door. It was RC—a guy who lived upstairs and a friend of the family. He asked if I wanted to work because Uncle JW had told him I was looking for work. So I left for work with him that same morning. There were a few older and younger guys going with us. RC had a painting contract on the North side. I was really glad to be working and making my way. Got along real well with all the other guys, and RC paid us after each day in cash. This was great; now I could buy things for Mom, Grandma, and Howard and contribute to the house like a man. It felt good.

When I got home, the first thing I did was to show Grandma what I had made and began to tell her what I was going to do with it. She cut me off and told me to sit down. She explained that Mom had passed away last night, and she had found her that morning after I had left.

Mom was gone now, and my days became gloomier and gloomier. I didn't want to stay at Grandma's anymore with the memories of my mom having passed away in the house and my not saying goodbye to her the morning I left. But if I left now, I'd be right back where I started going from "pillar to post" as Grandma often used. I had to maintain what I was doing now in hopes to become the man I should be. So I continued to live at home and work for RC; everything was going real well. But after a few months or so, RC began to get fewer and fewer contracts, and the workdays got to be less and less until it just about wasn't worth it anymore, so I stopped working with him. There were no hard feelings.

It was spring now, and summer was coming soon. It would be time for the watermelon wagons to roll out. That was a sure job without a doubt. Meanwhile, my older sister Maryann moved into the building where we lived. She and her boyfriend Bud had moved in together. I hadn't seen Maryann for a long, long time. I had never met Bud, but after I got to know him, we got along real well. I began to spend a lot of time at Maryann's apartment. My Uncle JW would always be there telling jokes and stories about his encounters but always had some funny and interesting things to tell. It was always a good time at Maryann's. And since I was sort of emancipated already, I was allowed to smoke and drink right along with them. And although Grandma smoked herself, you'd never catch me smoking in front of her and definitely not drinking.

Then one day, when I was at Maryann's, someone came to tell her that our cousin Herman had been killed. Herman was the only son of our Aunt Bessie Mae, our mother's sister, and Grandma's daughter Bessie Mae was the mother of our cousins Herman, Stella, Hermatte, Lucy, and Joann. Stella had sent for Maryann to come and identify Herman's body for her. She couldn't stand to do it herself. Mary Ann asked Uncle JW to go with her, but he didn't want to, so I volunteered. Maryann and I went to see Herman's body at the Cook County morgue.

An orderly took us to the basement; it was kind of cold and really dimly lit. As we walked, there were lots of metal drawers like those of a file cabinet. As we got to one section, there was a table with something on it covered with a white sheet. The orderly asked Maryann if was she ready. Then I knew it was Herman's body. He pulled the sheet back, and it was Herman. A portion of his skull was missing. His face was covered in blood, and from the imprint of the bottom of the sheet, you could tell that he had lost a foot. The orderly explained that he had been found on the elevated train tracks and had been run over by a train. Maryann didn't cry; she just stood staring for a moment, and so did I. Then we left and went back to Stella's house. Maryann talked with Stella, and we stayed a few days or so. Maryann went back home, and I stayed. After cousin Herman was buried, I continued to stay at Stella's house. Stella and her husband, John Bowden, who we all called BO worked during the day, so I would stay home with my cousins Hermatte, Lucy, Joann, Juanita, Pamela, and Bertina. Juanita, Pamela, and Bertina were Stella's daughters. We had lots of fun together and got into trouble with Stella at times. But they were so glad that they had a big cousin staying with them. Then one day, I found a stray puppy. He was a German shepherd. He wasn't so welcomed by Bo and Stella at first. But we were allowed to keep him if I would be responsible for him. I named him Duke. I'd take him with me when I would walk Hermatte to school.

Being there at Stella's house was good. There was often company with both friends and relatives. They would sort of party and play cards. I could occasionally have a beer, but I didn't mix with the adults. Bo would sometimes host a dice game. I didn't participate in those either. The children, we always stayed in the back room at those times. There was never any arguing or fighting. Staying at the house with the girls when Bo and Stella were at work or went out for a night wasn't like baby-sitting because all the girls were always well-behaved and always completed whatever chores they were given, and Hermatte was like the little mama. They always obeyed her just like they would Stella. So this gave me freedom to go out and hang out with a few friends I had made while staying with Stella on Lake Park.

It's funny that the friends I made were actually rival gang members, but we had never met one another in any of the gang fights. And I had let it be known that I was a member of the Del Viking street gang from Thirty-Fifth and State Street. The leader whose name was Kilroy had already known my cousins. So my affiliation with the Del Vikings made no difference to him. And we never talked gang talk. We just drank and socialized together. I even met his family who only lived about a block away. I'd still go back and forth to Thirty-Fifth Street to hang out. Sometimes, I would run into Val-mea, and late at night, I would bring her back with me and sneak her in through the back door. I knew about what time Stella and Bo would be asleep or out until two or three in the morning. And even when they'd come in, they were more than likely to go straight to bed, and if they got up later, it would be just to go to the bathroom. Even if they did go to the kitchen or from where the girls and I slept, they didn't pay too much attention to my bed across the room. And I would always make sure and have Val-mea out before they got up. The girls would never say anything even when they saw me come in with her or leaving out.

Then one day, Stella did catch Val-mea and I in bed; we had over slept. I thought she would be boiling mad. But she only said that we couldn't be sleeping together around the girls. And that it wasn't good because we were just teenagers, and it was disrespectful of me to just bring her into her house like I did. So that was the end of that. After I took Val-mea back to Thirty-Fifth that time, we sort of drifted apart. I didn't hang out on State Street as much and began hanging out more around Prairie and Giles with Bobo, Dwight, Fred, and Arthur and just working on the watermelon wagon. But soon, the Hughes decided to quit the watermelon business. The horses and wagons were all sold, and soon, the yard and barn were being torn down. The watermelon wagons helped keep a lot of young guys like myself out of trouble at times and provided a means of sustaining ourselves financially to keep us from robbing and stealing.

After that, I would spend a lot of time in the pool halls. There were two I would go to all the time, almost like a job. Because I could gamble and make money every day. I became real good at it even against some of the older guys. Later, it came to me that pool hustling wasn't such a promising way of support alone. As most of the older guys and even my friends had day jobs and could afford to lose games here and there because they had a paying job to make up their losses. So I searched the newspapers for jobs, but you had to be at least seventeen years old. I had at least a couple more years to go. So I remembered how guys would come into the pool halls selling all kinds of things and even selling walking up and down the streets. They seemed to be good at it and free to start and stop whenever they wanted to. Then it came to me about the shops around the Twelfth Street market, Jew town as we called it. There was a shop that sold watches cheap. I could buy some of them and sell them for a small profit. They looked expensive and had names similar to more expensive watches. I invested in some, and they were selling real good around the neighborhood for a while, then that played out.

Afterward, I found out about a job at a car wash on Forty-Seventh and Indiana owned by a guy called Poor Woods, never knew his real name. But he would come by occasionally dressed in nice suits and driving a new Eldorado Cadillac car. He'd always tell the guys how he came to own his car wash and a liquor store at Thirty-Fifth and Indiana Street. And that if we worked hard and stayed with him, we could make out real good and maybe start our own business one day soon. The job was fun, and all the guys got along good with each other. We got an hourly salary plus tips and bonuses now and then. The summer was great. But the winter started to disagree with me. I never really cared for the cold and snow. I quit and went back to hustling at the pool hall. Then I got word that my cousin David had come home from St. Charles Reformatory. Everybody was glad to see him back. He was still involved with the gang, but it was really noticeable that he had matured a lot. He was the same David when the chips were down, but a lot of his ways had changed.

Later, he and his girlfriend Brunetta became pregnant with their first child—a boy who they named after David. Brunetta was living at home with her mother at the time. Then a few months later, she and David moved in with his mom. Not long after they moved into their own apartment, a three-bedroom apartment, then came the era of Black awareness. Black people began expressing their Black African heritage through dress and culture. Processed and straightened hair were replaced by natural hairstyles, and African crafts and wares sprang up throughout the cities. David and I and several other of our friends began to shy away from the gang life and became interested in the various Black movements and African culture groups. We studied a lot of Black history books and literature. We attended many cultural Black entertainment venues. When we got together for exchange sessions, we mainly would meet at David's house.

Then one day, as I was just hanging out with a few of the brothers, I saw an older Black gentleman and a white guy peering through the window of a vacant store front. It had a for rent sign on it. And I was curious about what were they thinking of opening up there. I walked over to them and introduced myself. We had formed a sort of brotherhood among us, and I had chosen some African sounding names for us. I was Siheki; David was Ka-boo-lah. Bobo was Boo-ba-yah; Dwight was Day-ah-too while Fred was Fu-kee-bah, and Arthur was A-too-roh. Once introduced, the older gentleman explained that he and the other gentleman were trying to bring the idea of understanding and benefiting from economics to the Black communities. The majority of all the businesses in that area were Black-owned and operated. So I told Wilbur that I didn't think that it would be a good idea for the white guy to be in an office in the neighborhood at this time. Wilbur understood and said he and his friend worked together, and he wouldn't want to do it alone. Then he asked if I thought that anyone in the neighborhood might be interested in learning about economics. I told him yes if someone they knew was teaching it. So he asked if I would be interested. I said yes; he said he would pay the rent and utilities and pay me a weekly salary. I told him I would need someone to help me. He agreed and said he would pay them also.

So I told Cousin David about it. He agreed to help me. But we decided it would really be a waste of time trying to spread that through the community. We decided we would use the place for our gatherings and discussions of mutual interests between other Black groups and organizations. So we named the space "The Black Box." We had Wilbur's pamphlets and information on economics displayed in the window and had it set up inside, classroom style. We even had a loud speaker over the doorway that could be heard two to three blocks away. Once in a while, we would play recorded information in economics just in case Wilbur came by. But mostly, we played African music and speeches by Black leaders and jazz from time to time. I convinced Wilbur that the name Black Box and the music and speeches were only a means of attracting people to come in. And once they were in, they would be more receptive to the concepts of economics. Wilbur liked the idea. He would only come once a week to bring the money for David and I and bring more literature. Eventually, he stopped coming, and I would go to his house to pick up our money. Whenever he would pay the rent six months in advance, the utility bills would go directly to his house.

Well, everything was good. We had a place of our own to hold gatherings and meetings to further the expression of our Black awareness. We even had jam sessions as a few of us played musical instruments. When we would play music over the loudspeaker, people would stop and dance right in front of the shop. These were really fun times, then one day, as a few of the brothers and I were standing along Thirty-Fifth Street, there came two young ladies walking by on their way to a store. One of them really caught my eye. She had a fair brown complexion, quiet features, and she was slightly taller than me. She had her hair braided in sort of a backward style. She was just very pretty to me. She walked with a shyness to it. I just had to meet her. So I waited until she came back. On impulse, I reached out and grabbed her hand and asked her, her name. Still walking, she didn't snatch her hand away; she slowly pulled it away and looked at me with a half-smile and kept going. I asked if anybody knew her name. Bobo told me her name was Jean, and he pointed down the street on Giles and pointed out the house where she lived. He lived on the same street, just a few houses down across the street. On occasion, the brothers and I would congregate on Bobo's porch, sometimes singing some of the old Dustie's tunes of Black artists and groups.

From there, I could see Jean's house and sometimes catch a glimpse of her on the porch. I just really had to get to know her. I had girlfriends before, but there was just something about her quiet look. And she had sort of a relaxed innocence, so to speak. To me, she was unique. I would see her from time to time coming to and from the store; I'd speak, and she would just smile and wave while walking away. Then one day, I asked her if I could walk with her. She agreed but said I couldn't come up on her porch because her uncle and aunt didn't allow a lot of people hanging out on their porch. So when she got home, she went in and came back out. I was at the foot of the stairs. Then a couple of other people came out and sat and started laughing—the way young people do when they think you have a boyfriend or girlfriend. After a while, they left. Jean and I just talked general things, nothing personal. Then I left and went back to the corner. Almost every day from then on, I would see Jean, and we would walk and talk.

Eventually, one day, I met her uncle and aunt. They liked me, and I was allowed to come up and ask for Jean and sit on the porch with her. Then I met her mom and brothers; everyone seemed to approve of me. We started walking and talking together more. Jean started to come around the shop more and began to wear her hair up in a natural style. We began to spend more and more time together riding in different places. Dwight would borrow his mom's car after he had taken her to work. Jean and I and the other brothers and their girlfriends would even ride out to Dwight's grandmother's home in Harvey, Illinois, sometimes. To me, it was sort of like getting away from the everyday into a relaxed, free, and laid-back getaway.

The times were just so peaceful and happy all the time, never a worry or a problem. Then then sixties riots happened. More and more militant groups were springing up and speaking out. Turmoil became widespread throughout Chicago. There was vandalism, looting, and chaos everywhere. Thirty-Fifth Street was no different. Any white-owned business was fair game. Mayor Daley issued a shoot to kill order in Chicago. Offices of Black organizations were literally bombed and burned out even though the riots in Chicago were nothing like Detroit or the other cities. I had my part in it, getting whatever I could to share with my family. Whenever I would be visiting with Jean and there was a business being looted, I would leave and follow the crowd. And Jean would tell me not to go, and she worried that I might get hurt or caught by the police. I went anyway, but all the time thinking that she was the one girl I wanted to be with and that maybe it was time to slow my ways and get more serious about life.

After the atmosphere cleared and calmed, things went back to normal for us at the Black Box. Then one day, as we were just hanging out at the shop, a group of brothers passed by dressed in their African garments, and some had turbans on and books under their arms. They were passing out some sort of pamphlets. We approached them to find out what they were about because they had a certain air about them. They gave us some pamphlets to read. It was called the Freedom Concept. They explained that it was time for Black people to regain their true identity and reclaim their birthright. We invited them into our shop; the books they carried were Bibles. Once inside, we all sat around in a circle. They began to read scriptures and compare a lot of historical things to things happening at that time in America and how it has affected the lives of Black people and that it was time to leave America and not only return to Africa but also to the land of God—Israel.

Everything they read and said seemed to fit and make sense. They told us they met every Saturday at one of the group member's home at Thirty-Eighth and Indiana. We all agreed to go to one of their meetings to learn more of what they were about. The next few meetings, we took our ladies with us to meet the other sisters. Each meeting was more uplifting and inspiring than the first. We also learned that there were brothers and sisters from the group already living in Monrovia, Liberia, West Africa and had established their own community with a restaurant, ice cream shop, and all. At one of the meetings, we were introduced to a brother named Ben Ammi. He was the spokesman and leader of the group "The Black Hebrew Israelites." He further expounded on the history of the ancient Israelites and our spiritual connection to the land of Israel and our identity as God's chosen people. From then on, we identified with the Black Hebrew Israelites. We attended all meetings and functions. On Sundays, we would go down to the Twelfth Street market known as "Jew Town" and stand on milk crates that were called soap boxes and deliver our message on megaphones throughout the market. And hand out our leaflets of the freedom concept; there were audiences, black and white alike.

Then the meetings were getting smaller and smaller. That's because some people had made the trip to Liberia to live. At one meeting, brother Ben Ammi announced that it was now time to begin the journey to Israel and that in order for us to be able to finance the trip, everyone had to start saving their monies and pooling their resources. There also came the time that the brothers weren't able to keep the apartment where the meetings were held. And we began to hold meetings at the shop on Thirty-Fifth Street.

Not long after we lost the shop, I moved in with David and Brunetta. And during this time, Carolyn and her family had moved from Giles to a house on Prairie. I spent a lot of time visiting with Carolyn every day and spent a lot of time in the pool room hustling. Meanwhile, David had started a small business of his own. He was saving money for his trip to Israel. The group was holding meetings somewhere else, and David would ask me to come because the time was close to being ready to leave for Israel, and if I wasn't ready, I'd be left behind. Eventually, David and Brunetta were moving to another apartment and had begun selling some of their old furniture to help pay for their trip. My sister Maryann had moved into a nice coach house further south and offered me to come stay with her and her boyfriend Lee Walker; I did. Jean had become pregnant with our first child. Her mom wasn't aware of it 'til much later. Meanwhile, we would visit with David and Brunetta at their new apartment. David would urge me to continue to get ready and stay in touch because the time was getting close for everyone to start leaving, but I continued to skip meetings and became comfortable with my regular nonchalant ways, not taking it that serious.

Jean's mother moved from Prairie back to Giles street. When her mother found out about her pregnancy, she wasn't the usual angry, tantrum-throwing mom. She sat us both down and asked me what were my plans for taking care of Carolyn Jean and the baby. That, as funny as it seems, was the first time I knew that Jean was Carolyn Jean and not just Jean. I told her mother that I would get a job, and I wanted to marry Carolyn. It sort of worked the other way around. We wanted to get married right away; her mom agreed, but because Carolyn wasn't eighteen yet and I wasn't twenty-one, both our parents had to sign for us. My dad signed for me, and her mom signed for her. So we got married, and I lived with Carolyn and her mom and brothers.

Our son was born, and my cousin, Marvin David's, older brother got me a job at the steel mill. I worked the graveyard shift from 11:00 p.m. until 7:00 a.m., Monday through Saturday. Most days after work, I would just stay in with Carolyn and Melvin Junior until it was time to go back to work. As the brothers became scarce for hanging out with. Fred, Arthur, and Dwight had their jobs. Bobo was very close with David, and I hardly ever saw him; even when I went to his house, he was never home. I felt that I had blown it by not keeping up with the meetings and visiting David like I was. All Carolyn and I ever talked about since the birth of Melvin Junior was leaving America and getting to Israel so that our son wouldn't have to grow up with the hardships, the gang situations, the racism, and prejudices.

Months had passed since we had seen or even heard of a Hebrew brother or sister. Carolyn and I wondered how we would get out now. Then one day, I went to the newsstand to buy a paper which I would do from time to time, but this particular time, I was really glad I had bought the paper. The front page read that a large group of

Black Hebrews had left for Israel. My heart sank. I thought, *Carolyn and my child are doomed to stay and die in America now because of my ignorance. I had let my wife and child down. And I was supposed to take care of them. What was I going to do now?* I showed Carolyn the paper. She was shocked and disappointed. We were both sad; all this time, we had boasted to our families that we were leaving America for a better life, and they too should leave to save their lives and their children, and here we were, stuck here. Right at that moment, Carolyn and I had her mother watch the baby, and we hurriedly went to David and Brunetta's house. When we got there, we went up and knocked and knocked at the door. There was no answer. Then I leaned over the railing and looked in the window. I could see all the way from the living room to the back door that the entire apartment was empty. They were gone. Carolyn and I sat on the stairs awhile in disbelief that they had gone and left us behind.

As we went on with our lives still knowing that we had to get out of America as soon as possible, I kept on working and opened a bank account at the Drexel National Bank in the Lake Meadows Shopping Mall on Thirty-Fifth Street. We began saving our money praying that one day soon, we would find some other Hebrews to join that were going to Israel.

We still practiced the Hebrew culture and way of life ourselves. Soon, the steel mill began laying off workers. And now, Carolyn and I felt it was time for us to move into our own place because in her mom's apartment, we slept on the sun porch. That was all the room she had for us and the baby. It wasn't too bad. I weather-proofed it for the winter. So we had enough in our bank account for moving expenses as we had no furniture to worry about.

Now I would have to find another job. It wasn't easy. So in the meantime, we applied for "general assistance" where we would receive a check every month along with food stamps to buy groceries. We found a three-and-a-half-room apartment on Forty-Eighth and South Parkway. It wasn't the nicest of buildings in which to live, but it was what we could afford at that time. We lived there for a few months. Then we moved to Fifty-Third and Michigan Avenue. There were only single rooms available, there but it was a better neighborhood with nicer buildings. There, we had a very nice and very large room where we shared the bathroom and community kitchen with another couple down the hall.

We continued to practice the Hebrew culture and way of life. I began to study the Hebrew language for the day that we would be living in Israel. I would stay up very late into the night studying; we felt confident that *God* would eventually make a way for us to get to Israel. Then one day, my cousin Marvin who I had always kept in touch with came by our place. He had a job for me at a meat-packing company. This was a good opportunity for us to save even more money. Things were looking better for us. Then one day, I got the news that my aunt Ida had passed away. So I, being in the Hebrew culture, still decided to dress in a turban and a drape-like robe that I had made myself to attend her funeral. I got a lot of stares from most of the family I hadn't seen for quite some time. Carolyn didn't attend with me. I got a much-welcomed surprise to see that my cousin David had returned from Israel for his mom's funeral. Israel was like the other side of the world to me. I didn't get a chance to spend much time with him then, but he was going to be in America for a while, and he agreed we'd get together. Some time passed as there were lots of family for him to get around to.

Meanwhile, Carolyn and I had moved from our place to my sister Maryann's apartment at Fifty-Third and Calumet Street. I had called her to explain that we were trying to save money to go to Israel. She was eager to have us stay and was equally elated to have her first nephew, Melvin Jr. there with here. By this time, my job at Frigid Meats where Marvin had got me hired was over, and all we had to rely on now was our general assistance benefits. Maryann didn't ask for my rent, just to contribute to the groceries each month.

A few weeks or so later, a knock came at the door; it was David. He told us all about his trip to Israel and the country and how everyone was doing, and he told us what we would need to take with us. He took us around and helped us shop for the necessary things. Carolyn and I were ecstatic that our prayers had been answered to see someone again so we could finally have help to get to Israel. After David's daily visits with us during his stay in America, it was time for him to return to his family in Israel. His sister Avon and her daughter had also gone to Israel when the first group left. Before he left, he said he felt we would be better off staying close to the group so we wouldn't be left behind this time. He introduced us to a brother he trusted; we would be well off to stay with. He informed us of a place where meetings were being held. We stayed with Maryann awhile longer and later moved in with the brother whose Hebrew name was Nathaniel and his wife and son on the very far south side. By this time, Carolyn was pregnant with our second son, Samuel.

The meetings David told us about were being held in a print-shop on Forty-Third and Vincennes Avenue owned by a brother named LA Bryant. Brother Bryant had been a Baptist minister before, and when he would speak before our congregation, it would always be inspiring and enlightening and full of life. He didn't speak of the teachings of the church; he spoke about the position and plight of Black people in America and around the world. From time to time, there would be speakers who had been to Israel and came back to report to us how others were doing that were now living there. And we would see films of the brothers and sisters moving about in the land and different places in the land that were spoken of in the Bible. It was all so inspiring and beautiful. I had to get my family there, no question about it. It was definitely time to put my all in all and one thousand percent into it.

At this time, I felt that since the brothers that had come from Israel had Hebrew names, it was time that Carolyn and I and our children have Hebrew names as well. I searched the Bible and found a name that I thought was fitting for Carolyn, so I named her Anim. Myself, I named Shamoor. Melvin Jr. I named Shamoor also. I hadn't known how to say junior in Hebrew yet. And we would wait to name our second child. After each meeting, a collection was taken up. This was to help the printshop which now, instead of printing for the public, was printing solely for us.

Brother Bryant was now promoting the Hebrew cause and rallying support for us even from political figures in the United States government and internationally, including Africa. The printshop became the RGOI headquarters (the Representative Government of the Immigrants). Letters and documents were mailed out daily. The collections also served as a means of helping families with their plane fares to Israel. Everyone contributed what they could each week. Every couple of months or so, an announcement would be made that a family had been chosen to leave for Israel. Each week, everyone eagerly waited and prayed to hear their name called. At this point, we no longer considered ourselves just a group or organization. We were the "Black Hebrew Israelite" nation as we had become more recognized and accepted as a thriving and positive example for Black people in America. Our speaking engagements had now far surpassed that of the days on the soap boxes on Twelfth Street.

They were now expanded to schools and other institutions and halls. The responses were positive and promising. We held social gatherings and put on our own entertainment for ourselves and the public. We performed our own wedding ceremonies (Hebrew weddings). I was placed in charge of securing blank marriage licenses which we would buy from Rosenblum's Jewish bookstore on the north side. The licenses were printed in Hebrew which I had learned to read, write, and speak fairly well. I translated the licenses to brother Bryant who performed the ceremonies. Before long, Brother Ben Ammi sent for Brother Bryant to get up to Israel as soon as possible. But before he left, he introduced three brothers to us who would keep everything together and moving ahead in his absence. The brothers were Brother Warren Brown, Edgar Brinson, and Jerome Copeland. They had been very instrumental in working directly with brother Bryant in a lot of endeavors that helped to further and strengthen the support of our cause. After Brother Bryant's departure, the printshop closed. But our meetings carried on at a local YMCA on Fiftieth and Indiana.

Then I was appointed as the Hebrew language teacher since we were moving to Israel and that was the language of the country. So we set up once a week classes, and I was paid $5 per person. Actually, I was learning as I taught. During this time, we named our second son Shmuel. Later, we weren't able to hold our meetings and classes at the YMCA anymore. So the brothers rented rooms at the Roberts Motel at Sixty-Fifth and Martin Luther King Jr. Drive. Then at one particular meeting, we were told that there had started to be some problems with some of us entering the country (Israel), and we were being turned back. It had a lot to do with some of the brothers and sisters not being able to stick to a very carefully planned script of why we were coming to Israel. Strange enough, some people got in while others were yet turned away. So this meant a waste of monies from time to time. Later, it sort of eased up.

The brothers felt the need to step up the departures of the brothers and sisters. But this meant that we needed to raise monies fast. So one of the brothers had a brother who owned a travel agency in downtown Chicago; he convinced his brother to go along with a planned hold up in which the agency would be robbed of hundreds of airline tickets and be given to someone who could fill them in as needed and be channeled through a particular airline. His brother would receive the insurance from the robbery. So myself and another brother enlisted to carry this out. We displayed empty, weapons but no one was ever hurt. The brother and I were back home in time to see ourselves on the news driving away from the scene as police cars converged on the agency from every direction. The incident was never spoken of in any of the meetings. It was only said that we had been blessed with a way to begin to move more families to Israel faster.

It was a blessing because my family and I were the very next ones to be chosen to go along with a few other brothers and sisters, and we were going to meet a few more once we arrived at the airport (O'Hare). Brother Brown explained that I would be in charge and for everyone to follow my instructions especially when we got to Israel. Because of my knowing some of the language enough to communicate with airport authorities there, this might somehow be a plus in neutralizing our position. After meeting the others, we were on our way. Everyone was so happy. After a while, I heard an announcement that we would be landing in Amsterdam. I first thought maybe we had made a mistake. Then I learned it was just a connection stop to pick up other passengers also traveling to Israel, whew! That was a big relief. Then we were on our way. It didn't seem that we had been flying that long, and it seemed that we had flown from day into night. Then I learned of the time zone difference.

Finally, we were awakened by the announcement that we would be landing at Israel's Tel Aviv airport shortly. Once we landed and disembarked, I had already been told at which gate we would be met. Speaking in Hebrew, I asked for instructions how to get there. Once there, I spoke and translated at the passport checkpoint. We got the all clear. All of our passports were stamped with a visa of six months as was the customary time allotted for our stay. But many of us had already been there much longer. As we crossed the gates toward exiting the airport, we saw a group of brothers there to greet us. In front of them was Brother Bryant. I greeted Brother Bryant with a handshake and an embrace; he then told us his name now was Sha-lee-ahk.

Once outside the airport, we all were loading into two flat trucks. What a time we had laughing and talking and getting acquainted with the others and trying to see what we could of Israel through the dark. In about half an hour, we arrived in a city called Arad; we were taken into sort of like a row house. There, we were greeted by lots of brothers and sisters as well as children. Everyone was very happy to see us and came up to introduce themselves without hesitation. We all conversed and exchanged experiences, etc. through until daybreak. Then it was time to get back in the trucks and move on.

Brother Shaleak explained that we were going to "Dimona." That's where we would be staying. The scenery was awesome—the grassy hills and mountains, the valleys, and the skies were the bluest I had ever seen. It was September, but it felt like mid-July. The buildings didn't look too much different than those I had seen in America. The cars and buses were a little different. Once at Dimona, we pulled into a parking lot to an apartment complex. We were greeted by a crowd of brothers and sisters and children once again. It was like we had been on a long journey for years and had finally returned home. The greeting was so warm and heartfelt. We went inside the complex. There was a big courtyard.

There were brothers and sisters, old and young, walking about, sitting and talking; some seemed to be studying. Some of the brothers were playing chess. The children were running and playing. There were a few Israeli people passing by here and there. And some, even at their windows, were looking out into the courtyard. I could hear them speaking Hebrew. I could understand a little of what they were saying. It seemed they were talking one hundred miles an hour. I said to myself that I would be speaking like them in no time, studying and hearing it every day. Then I saw one of the brothers that had come to America and spoke to us at the printshop. I was about to approach him to speak to him. But one of the other brothers stopped me and told me he was an outcast now. He had disagreed with the appointment of princes who would be the governing body of our nation. I wasn't allowed to speak to him. I learned that there were to be twelve princes besides Ben Ammi who was already the accepted head prince. There wasn't yet twelve princes, and they were still being chosen.

My family and I were taken to an apartment in the complex. This was Ben Ammi's apartment where he lived with his three wives. It was our teaching that the men were allowed to have multiple wives in accordance with the laws of the Old Testament which we lived by. We were going to be living there until we could be placed elsewhere. I asked where my cousin David and Avon were. I was told they lived in a different city called Mitzpe Ramon.

That next day, the family and I were driven there. Everyone we had known from the neighborhood that was a part of the nation in the states were there. We received the same joyful reception that we had when we first had arrived. We were just going to be there temporary until our permanent place in Dimona was ready. While there, I was shown where David and Avon lived, but we had to be announced first. That's when I knew that David had also been chosen to be one of the princes. Now he was called Nasee Ben Daveed (Prince Ben Daveed). I and the family were taken to his apartment. He and Brunetta were so glad to see us. He showed me around the city along with some of the other brothers. We walked up to a high area where you could actually see eagles flying around. We walked along a sort of narrow path around a mountain where it seemed like thousands of feet below was a crater, quite scary, but they were used to it. We all sat down along the path and exchanged conversations about our experiences in the States and now how it felt to actually be in the biblical promised land where the Hebrews of old had walked. For me, it was a feeling of pure relief and joy; I literally teared up.

It was drawing near two o'clock, and everyone was going in for a while. They told me it was "Haf-see-kah" time. This was the time that all shops closed and everyone went on to rest for a couple of hours. So Daveed and I went in. Brunetta and Anem were preparing lunch for everyone. While we were waiting, Daveed told me about enema cleansing and the health benefits of it. Although Carolyn and I didn't eat pork, we still ate other meats. And now, we were becoming vegetarians. And an enema would help to clean our stomach walls and digestive tract. But that it wasn't necessary to do it right away. So later, we began to do the enema cleanses every couple of weeks or so. Brunetta's name was changed to "Sarah," and Avon was now "Bot-zion."

For entertainment, there was a small theatre in the area we would go to every now and then. It was a small place; seemed like it was just thrown together with folding chairs for seats and one guy using a movie projector of some kind. The movies were as old as we were. A guy came one day and asked for someone to take a night job to watch and keep some kind of motors going that supplied electricity to something on the mountain. It didn't pay much, but I took it as the little money that Anim and I had was running low, and all we had to look forward to for finance was basically monies sent from our families from time to time.

To pass the time, some days, a few of the brothers would get together with their musical instruments they had brought over with them and have a music session out in one of the groves nearby. There was a conga drum available, and I would join in as best as I could as I didn't really know how to play. We'd go out too; sometimes three times a week and practice looking forward to the day we would have a real band to perform throughout Israel. A couple of the brothers had played with bands before in the States. We stayed with Daveed a few months more before we moved back to Dimona. Not long after we got back, my Hebrew was getting better and better. And Shaleak who was also a prince now had an extensive knowledge of the history of Israel, and world history had begun taking brothers and sisters on tours throughout the land. Nasee (prince) Shaleak wanted me to go along to sort of translate for him when needed. We visited the old city of Jerusalem and many biblical sites. We went through Jericho. It was amazing to me to see so many Black people dressed in cultural garb. I later learned they were Arab. Some were even dressed in western clothes. I could hear them speaking a language that wasn't Hebrew. I saw signs written in some strange script. I really felt good about Jericho. I wondered what it would be like to live there speaking their language with them.

When we got back, I told Nasee Shaleak about it. He said he would speak to Nasee Ben Ammi. Ben Ammi thought it would be good for me and could very well be beneficial for our communities in the future. So not long after my family and I were moved to Jericho, Nasee Ben Ammi had rented us a small villa there. We loved it. In our yard, we had different fruit trees. The market was only right up the street. It was the custom for a tea salesman to bring fresh mint tea to your house.

I'd walk to the mountains each morning exploring new places. The views were breathtaking. I explored some abandoned clay-built houses, seemed they had bullet holes all over them. I later learned that was a result of the six-day war conflict between Israel and the Arabs. I would take bus rides to Jerusalem to shop from time to time. In December, I would be standing in my yard in a T-shirt and shorts and see a snow-covered bus pull up from Jerusalem; people would get off with their coats on. Yet the sun was hot and shining in Jericho. It was something to see. Nasee Ben Ammi would send us money each week by truck with one of the brothers. We lived in Jericho for several months; while there, I had begun to learn the Arabic language pretty well.

Then one day, we were told it was time for us to return to Dimona because some sort of conflict between Israel and the Arabs was brewing, and it wouldn't be safe for us. When we returned to Dimona, some new arrivals had come; among them was Brother Shakor and his wife Le-shee-ma who we had known in Chicago, and we were going to share an apartment. Later, Anem had become pregnant with our third child, and we were going to need more space. So we were moving into a larger apartment with a brother named El-kanon and his wife T'hee-lah and their children.

El-kanon was a leather craftsman; he made belts, sandals, purses, carrying bags for the brothers and sisters, and lots of other crafts. The communities began to grow and grow, and the Israeli government began to stop the entry of some of the people into Israel. They began to search out and deport many of us. Later, Nasee Ben Ammi and the princes devised a way for some of the brothers and sisters to get into the country undetected by the government. And also, we were able to send brothers out to continue to bring others into the nation and, eventually, into the land.

Meanwhile, we continued to establish and build our communities in Israel. Now all the princes had been chosen. And there were ministers chosen with different responsibilities. There were those in the community that had experience in different fields such as medical and holistic health. Anem studied and became one of the doctors. She was very good at it. We established a school. We named it "The Kingdom School" as our mission was to establish and bring the kingdom of God into its glory. Children were divided by age into grade levels; teachers were chosen and assigned from among those who had previous experience or knowledge of certain subjects. Because of my basic knowledge of the Hebrew language, I was chosen as Hebrew teacher to all grades. I even held classes for the adults. I was also chosen to help organize, create, and institute the curriculum. A brother named Ahm-rahm was appointed the minister of education; his wife Yo-yah-dah was appointed the deputy minister of administration. Not very long after, I was appointed the principal. From there, I was appointed the deputy minister of operations. Larger classes were being held in one of the bomb shelters (basement) under the complex. Also, during this time, we had formed a band which I and Brother Shakor, whose name was changed to Anaviyah, became members of. Playing the conga drums, Anaviyah's wife, Le-shee-mah (her name changed to Y'shee-bah) became one of the school's teacher. The children were transported to and from school daily from the other two cities. We soon had school uniforms and our own national anthem. Textbooks were sent to us by the brothers on mission in the States. I was in charge of securing any Hebrew materials to be used in the school. We slowly began to teach almost all of our classes in Hebrew. Some of the houses allowed their living rooms to be used as class-rooms during the day. Then they were transformed back after school hours. The two flat vans we had transported children to and from school each day, brought food from the markets to all three cities, and took our band, singers, and dance troupes to and from perfor-mances. During this time, the Israeli government had sort of eased on the deportations and allowed us to exist in peace and move about. It became an issue of world opinion to them.

During this time, our third child was born. It was a boy. We named him Ze-ra-kee-yah. He was a sort of struggling baby from the onset. Anem would sit up nights with him calming his crying and sometimes soothing what seemed like discomfort. It was an off and on thing. Finally, Anem enlisted the help of some of the other doctor sisters. They all tried their best to get him better, but to no avail, he passed away. I had always felt that he should've been taken to Beersheva, to the hospital. I had said it many times, but who knows, maybe even then would have been too late. I never blamed anyone, especially not Anem. Some had been saved in the past, and some passed away. As doctors today can know the problem but just can't fix it no matter how much learning they have. This was a very sad chapter in our lives, and even now, replaying this as I write is really a chore.

So Zerakiyah was buried, and Anem and I got through it know-ing that our other two sons would grow up happy and healthy and that we would be blessed again. Things finally got back to normal for us. And the nation was still thriving and growing. We got word that a new group of people had arrived. Some of the brothers were saying there were a lot of single sisters among them. They were anxious to go up and meet them. I hadn't been thinking of taking another wife as yet. After about a week, during school hours, some new children were brought to Dimona to attend. I noticed in my Hebrew class that two of the new students were really advancing fast. I was really amazed at their progress in such short time. They were two little girls (sisters) Bina and B'hee-rah; they were little power house of learning. I thought they must have a really great and caring mom. Oh yeah, they had two brothers, Nay-aman and Z'maree-yah. They were the opposite, but nothing I couldn't handle. They soon straightened out.

The girls reported back to me that their mom wondered what my technique was to get those two in learning order. I finally got a chance to meet their mom. Her name was Adee-vah; she had come to Dimona for a sisters meeting. I recognized her from the description the girls had given me. I guess they were in the market for a dad. I went to introduce myself, and she said, "You must be Shamoor. The girls talk about how such a good teacher you are, and they like your class better than any." I was impressed. After the meeting, I waited for her and walked her out to the van where she was returning to Arad. From then, we would walk and talk when she came to Dimona, and sometimes, if the van was going to Arad, I would catch a ride. Well, we got to know each other well, and after a few months, I asked her to be my wife. She agreed.

Anem had seen and heard of us together and her and Adeevah often walked and talked, so my intentions were well-known. It was not that any sister had a say in whether a brother could take another wife or any particular wife, but it was important that they could get along like sisters. But still, there was a deciding factor to this. As we also had a priesthood order that instituted a sort of courting period called Mee-koo-deh-shet—a period of sanctity which lasted seventy days to see if the couple were actually compatible. During this period, the woman is allowed to cook for the man, do some laundry. They both can spend quality time with each other unsupervised; they can hold hands but no sexual embracing, no kissing on the lips, and definitely *no sex*! If any of these were disobeyed, the priests could terminate the Mee-koo-deh-shet, and there would be no marriage between the two. Then they both would be punished by not allowing them to marry anyone else for an unspecified amount of time until Nasee Ben-Ammi, being consulted with by the priests, lifted the punishment.

Well, Adeevah and I were finally married. It was customary for newlyweds to be sent on a honeymoon. The place was mostly chosen by Nasee Sha-lee-ak and Nasee-Ben Ammi. They were always nice places. The couples would be given enough money to enjoy themselves for a week however they wanted. The hotel or resort was already pre-paid. We spent ours in the old city of Jerusalem seeing the sites, visiting holy places, and shopping. It was a great time.

When we returned, Nasee Ben Ammi had arranged for me to receive a weekly salary for teaching. Before, he would always give each family monies each week to help out until the head of the family could find work around the city. Money was being sent in from the brothers in the States and the performances of the band. We had created our own store, and we would buy leather goods from El-kanon. This helped to keep most of the money within our communities. I had no complaints. My family was being taken care of, and we were all happy and healthy.

Anem was pregnant again with our fourth child; it was a girl. We named her Yeef-ah—the most beautiful bundle of joy we could ever had wished for. Now I had five sons and four daughters. It made me proud. When we all would go out walking or would sit in the park together, everyone would compliment us on how beautiful and happy we seemed. It was true! We were often seen as the model family. Nasee-sha-lee-ak was seen sort of as the second-in-command under Nasee Ben Ammi and his representative in certain matters.

There was a call for a special meeting. Normally, each city held their own meetings if it was not concerning the whole nation. So this was a nation meeting. Only the princes and ministers were called in from the other cities, and they would relay the results to the people in their cities. Sha-lee-ak began the meeting by giving all praises to the Most High God of Israel, then he began to read certain scriptures relating to the life, characteristics and deeds of Jesus, and his closeness with God. He likened those scriptures to the attributes and modern day works of Ben-Ammi whose name, when translated, means "son of my people." Sha-lee-ak continued reading scriptures that pictured Ben Ammi to be no different from Jesus and the prophecies of His resurrection. He then said that we shall no longer refer to Ben-Ammi as Nasee Ben Ammi but instead Nasee-Ha-Shalom, meaning, "the prince of peace." And that the twelve princes were as the twelve disciples who sat in counsel with Jesus. Each of the twelve princes had certain attributes that were said to sum up the spirit of Nasee-Ha-Shalom. From then on, that's what Ben Ammi was called.

Anytime you wanted to talk to him now, you would stand in a line outside of his door and wait to be announced. The princes were the only ones who could go straight into it; it was the new order of things, but no one minded it. Everything was still just as happy and joyous as ever until, one day, tragedy struck my family again. This time, it was our daughter Bina. She had gotten sick; it was never determined from what, but once again, the nation doctors tried to get her well, but it was to no avail. It paralyzed our whole family for a good while; Bina was always full of fun and vigor and just so lovable. In my leisure time, she always hung out with me; she was so precious. I took it very hard, and Adeevah took it doubly hard. Some days, her I and the boys and B'hira would walk and talk about our memories of her. At this point now, I'm thinking that we, the nation, need to start going to the hospital when people get sick because what we were doing just wasn't working. But you didn't dare defy the order of things. You didn't want to be cast out. And it would mean without your family. So you dealt with it as best you could.

Soon, things began to get better, and the family moved on with our lives. The nation continued on with our functions, celebrations, and gatherings. After a while, Nasee-Ha-Shalom sent for Adeeva. He was sending her to the States on a mission. Missions could last several months and sometimes a year or two. I understand that it was important that she go, but she would be deeply missed. She would send letters, pictures, and different things that the family wanted whenever someone was coming in from the States. We were all proud that Nasee-Ha-Shalom had the confidence in her to assist the brothers in their mission. There were plenty of things going on to keep us all busy during her absence. But yet every time it was announced that some people were coming in, we hoped and prayed she would be among them.

Meanwhile, a new group came in one day, and once again, one of the sisters caught my eye. I was reluctant to return a receptive eye because she looked like she was too young even though she had a daughter with her. Her name was Sha-veev-yah. Her daughter's name was Ohay-vee-yah. I asked some of the brothers who had come in with her if she was older than she looked, not so much. She displayed an innocent radiance to me.

One day, as I was standing reading a Hebrew newspaper, she walked up to me and started asking me things about the nation and the land. We began to talk more about her and where she was from in the States. She would come to my Hebrew classes, and I would spend extra time with her trying to teach her the language. We started to taking walks more and more getting to know each other. Again, my intentions to be together with her was in the open. Anem became close with her just as she did with Adee-vah, and Ohay-vee-yah blended right in with our other children. And also, Anem had bore our fifth child who we named Yah-keen. As he grew, he was just a wonder full of energy and surprise all the time.

Sha-veev-yah and I spent a lot of time together, but my time was equally spent with my family. Sha-veev-yah would come to all events that I participated in, and I would do the same with her. Then at times, I would notice that prince Rock A-meem had started to find occasion to always end up next to her; at various times, I couldn't tell what he would be talking about, but I could see in her expression that she didn't want to hear whatever it was. I didn't read too much into it. But later, it came out that he had feelings for her. I had never seen a brother trying to win a sister's attention when it's clear that she enjoys the attention of another brother. She even mentioned it to me herself. If that wasn't enough, he even approached me and said I was spending too much time with her, and it would make me lose sight of my purpose. I had enough! So I mentioned it to Nasee Shaleak who then was like my spiritual father (Dad); he said he would take care of it. He returned to me a day or so later and told me Nasee Rockameem had been reprimanded and all was well and not to worry. Nasee Rockameem never interfered again and never showed anger toward me.

Shaveevyah and I entered into M'koo-deh-shet and were married; we had a very memorable honeymoon. We had organized baseball and basketball teams from within for our recreation. Our basketball team was so good that we accepted and won a game against Israel's top team: "The Maccabees." We also ran track played soccer. These we played amongst ourselves. I did participate in baseball and many times came out the star of the game with my "split and catch" style on the field (doing a split while I catch the ball).

We always had joyous and happy times, but tragedy and illness were no strangers to us. There was the time when Minister Ahmram fell ill. He was moved out of the complex to another apartment we rented outside of the complex. His wife Yoya-dah and their family remained. I hadn't known what his illness was until Nasee Ha-Shalom sent for me and explained that he had, had a nervous breakdown, and his mind was gone. Here again, he wasn't taken to a hospital. But yet left to exist as best the nation knew how to care for him. I was asked to tend to him from time to time along with a couple other brothers; we were taking daily shifts caring, feeding, and keeping watch on him. The doctors would come in and clean him. I would try and get him to talk about school memories or anything he could associate with. Nothing helped, and he later passed away.

Then there was the case of Nasee Asiel's (Brother Brown) wife, Reev-kah. I had known her in the States. She was a strong vibrant sister, full of life. I had heard talk of her being ill but didn't know to what extent until again I was asked to take shifts with other brothers to walk her into the mountains to sit with her while she sunbathed. She had breast cancer. The mountains were rugged and slightly high, so it would be sort of difficult for a sister to hold her up and tread up the mountain. Eventually, she too passed away.

Here, I'll stop with the illnesses and deaths as they were numerous, but this is not the intent of the content of my story. So for more recreation for us, Nasee-Ha-Shalom purchased a horse. Not just any horse but a cold black Arabian Stallion purchased from the Bedouin Arabs. They had already named him Sa-Ar (Storm); he was fiery. We built a small barn for him. It had a small window cut out where the children could walk up and feed him. I had experience with horses, so I was elected to feed and care for him. Mostly, all the other brothers were sort of afraid of him. I would take him out for short walks daily talking to and calming him. We sort of bonded. But he was still that fiery stallion.

Then Nasee-Ha-Shalom thought maybe if he had company, it would change him, so we got another horse. But Sa-ar didn't get along with him always kicking and biting at him. So we all (the brothers) were asked which one to keep. It was a toss-up because maybe the children could enjoy riding the other horse as he was much gentler. But Sa-ar was pure blooded and would be good for siring good and valuable offspring. Sa-ar won! Well, the day had come for Sa-ar's big debut. We were celebrating what we called New World Passover. We would go to the tree groves where we held our sports events and other outings. Now was the time to show off Sa-ar. I was nominated to handle him. He'd jerk and rear-up occasionally but nothing drastically wild! To make it interesting, it was agreed that whichever brother would ride him in full gallop would be given one hundred shekel. There was no betting; we didn't gamble. There were no takers except one: *me*! We didn't have a saddle, so I would ride bare back. I did. Sa-ar was really, really fast. I won the one hundred shekels, and from then on, I was affectionately called the Little Giant when I would participate in certain events. Well, it was good I got a chance to ride Sa-ar, and he could show what he could do. Because one morning, I went out to feed and walk him, but he was gone. The barn had been broken into overnight. We never got another horse after that. All in all, that was a very memorable new world Passover for me.

And just when I thought things couldn't get any better, the next year, at the Passover celebration, the best things that could ever happen now happened. Adeevah had returned with another group of brothers and sisters. She introduced me to a beautiful sister named Ta-Ameen-yah. She said this is your Baht (daughter) meaning that Ta-Ameen-Yah had adopted Adeevah as her spiritual mom, although Ta-ameen-yah was grown, just as I had adopted Nasee Sha-lee-ak as my spiritual dad.

Lots of brothers were awestruck with her. Many made sure she noticed them. She and Adeevah were trying to make their way to our spot so she could meet the rest of the family. We all were so happy to have Adee-vah back home. It was a beautiful celebration. Afterward, a few brothers wanted to show her around the areas of the complex. But she declined and said she wanted me to show her around. I did. Then Nasee Sha-lee-ak asked me to walk her to where she'll be staying. A few of the brothers had seen us and said it had looked like I was taking all of the sisters that come in. Although our way of life permitted brothers to have seven wives, my three was quite enough for me, and whether anyone believed it or not, I genuinely looked on Ta-Ameen ya in the spirit of a father to a daughter. It wasn't hard to do because I was genuinely happy and satisfied with my wives and family even though I could sense a small bit of resentment from time to time. I still maintained my close relationship with her. But I was overjoyed when it was announced that she was going into M'koo-deh-shet with a brother named Mock-shu-riel—a very good brother for her. He was a craftsman and made fine jewelry for all the brothers and sisters. They were finally married. Hallelujah! Now the suspicions could be put to rest.

The nation wasn't only growing from people coming in from the States as Prince Ben-daveed and Prince Asiel would many times travel extensively back and forth to Africa. People from different African States would sometimes come to Israel to see what we were all about so that they might give their support to us. And there were some who knew and came to live among us. Oftentimes, Nasee-Ha-Shalom would send me to the airport to meet and escort them to Arad which was like our receiving city before they would come to Dimona to meet him and all the princes and people. The exchange between our nation and many African government grew so big that it was a must to train and send others to assist Nasee Asiel and Nasee Ben-daveed because they were also in charge of getting the people from the States to Israel and supplying and maintaining the finances to be sent home. So Nasee Sha-lee-ak came up with a training program. It came to be called the School of the Prophets. Brothers learned to be educators, economists, agriculturists, doctors of holistic and modern medicines, and many more fields. They were to be sent out to teach as well as learn.

Nasee Sha-lee-ak had collaborated on and written a book *God the Black Man and Truth*; a test would be given to the brothers based on the book. Those who passed the test would be deemed qualified to go out and represent the nation. I was chosen to make up the test. I made it as difficult as possible. Even some of the smartest brothers struggled with it. As it was in the beginning, people came, and people would leave it as it just wasn't for everybody. There was sort of an unplanned balance. But even so, there were a lot of us, and the complex begin to get crowded even with the extra apartments we had outside of it.

By the grace and blessing of God, the ingenuity and efforts of the princes and the willingness of the Israeli government, we were given some unfinished housing at the edge of the city close to the mountains; they were low-level housing that were going to be for immigrants. The mayor and the housing authority agreed we could have them rent free for a number of years if we would finish them ourselves. That wasn't going to be much of a problem because a lot of the brothers had come over with lots of skills. There were carpenters, brick layers, electricians, plumbers, landscapers, and more.

A meeting was called, and it was explained that some of the larger families would get their homes first then smaller families and next would be couples with no children then single people; the larger families were asked to go up and pick out their home first. The houses built were spacious, not too close together and not too far apart. There were a few that were built side by side so that if you wanted to join them to make one house, it wouldn't be that hard.

Nasee-Ha-Shalom had seen which houses the families had picked out. And he had the say as to which house to get ready first. His house was first. The skilled brothers—the electricians, carpenters, and plumbers—left at sunup to head out to the area to start work on the house. They would return late evening. I would walk up to the site every now and then on some of my regular walks to the mountains as I liked to do when I'm studying. The Na-see's house was coming along good. The grounds around it were cleared and flattened. Once it was time to start on the other houses, all the houses had been built on the mountain with fairly rocky and uneven ground. When it was time for the other houses except for the internal work, the families had to do the work around their houses themselves. Eventually, everyone was moved in; everyone brought what little furniture and belongings they had. Some didn't have furniture because they had lived with other families who were already established when they arrived. So they had to buy what they could from market places or from people selling through ads in the paper. The same was true even for Nasee-Ha-Shalom and the princes and ministers. On occasions, if you could pay, the carpenters would make what you needed. They had to travel out of the city for materials.

Sometimes, when we bought furniture from the marketplaces and even from people advertising, we had to clear bedbugs from them by scrubbing the piece down then spraying with kerosene and letting them sit in the sun for sometimes a week or more before we could bring them into our houses. Inside the house, there were two bedrooms, a bath with shower, a nice-sized kitchen with a back door, and a nice-sized living room, and a small terrace-like rear porch. It had been painted and did have the kitchen appliances in it already. It was nice to have your own home. I had a separate bedroom for myself. The three wives slept in the other bedroom, and all the children used the living room to sleep at night. The marital arrangement was that the wives would divide a month between them and schedule whose week it was to spend time with me that month. When one of them was on their cycle, they couldn't enter my room, wash, or cook for me or the family. It was considered their time of uncleanness. It was also sort of like a break for them. Also, they could not enter the kitchen. This was the rule in all marriages.

I never saw the whole inside of Nasee-Ha-Shalom's who, by this time, had become to be referred to as "rabbi" pronounced "Rah-bee" by us ("my spiritual leader"). But we learned it to be my master, my father, free-translated through our teachings. His house was referred to as "the rock" as in the rock of salvation. Here, he lived with his three wives and children. There came a time when we were expecting some diplomats to visit us at what we had now named the K'far, meaning "the village." In many ways, it did resemble a village.

The diplomats were due to arrive in a couple of months. And it was stressed that every house must be immaculate and orderly, and the families must make a good impression on the guests. Since the areas around the houses were bare of grass and flowers, we were instructed to plant both. I traveled to the city of Beersheba and bought packets of grass and flower seeds, and my three wives and I and all the children worked every day to get the grass and flowers to grow. Flowers began to come up slowly. The grass was growing but patchy. The end result wasn't too appealing. But we kept trying. Then one day, while I was standing outside my front door, I saw a large truck pull up beside Ra-bee's house. It had rolls and rolls of sod on it and flat crates of pre-potted flowers of all kinds. There were groups of brothers digging and raking all around his house. I couldn't believe that he had the people toiling in the hard mountain dirt trying to plant and grow grass and flowers while he was having his trucked in. His house wass bigger now and going to look better than the rest.

Okay, he is the spiritual leader, our godhead, so to speak. He began to be reverenced and referenced and liken to God. I respected him and was dedicated to the purpose of our mission here in God's land and admired that he had, in fact, accomplished what no man had against the odds and adversities. But I couldn't see him as godlike. But there were those you could tell no different, or you were the devil's servant. It was almost like treason to question or disagree with him even to your own family.

It had been agreed with the mayor and housing authority that we would have any amount of years before we would start paying rent. But no one knew or was really concerned with how long; after a while, it seemed like it was forgotten. The majority of the brothers acquired jobs. Trucks of contractors would show up often looking for workers. Even some of the sisters including two of my wives Adeevah and Sha-veev-yah went to work. All workers had to give 10 percent of their wages to the economists of the nation for whatever Rah-bee would need it for, not that he used it for himself. But it was not known to me, and I'm sure others, where it was used because there were several outlets which also provided monies for the nation including the States and Africa.

Soon, a decree was sent out and read house to house in regards to the rent. It read that all heads of households must pay rent of a certain amount every month starting the coming week, and if the rent isn't met, then the brother who has not paid cannot stay in the house until rent is paid up. For various reasons, some of the brothers hadn't paid and were literally put out of their homes to work and stay elsewhere and not come back into the village until they had the money. At this time, I was selling cassettes and albums of our music at all the performances, and Rah-bee was giving me 10 percent, and I was still head of the school and received weekly pay from that. I was saving and accumulating my monies.

As the band traveled, sometimes, we'd spend a couple of nights or even a week in another city. No one was supposed to, but I did. I opened a bank account in three different cities just in case I was out and had an emergency. Rah-bee controlled one bank account in Dimona for all the nation's financial transactions. Elderly people's checks such as social security, etc. were sent into that account. Then they were given money by Rah-bee from their check. The same was true for everyone. The princes and minister didn't work and were supported by the nation.

Anyway, when a few brothers couldn't pay their rent, I had it, so I helped them out. And being in charge of copying our music cassettes, I showed them how to invest with me in buying blank cassettes and being able to receive their money back in one or two weeks with a profit.

It didn't matter what the weather was, cold and raining or what, no rent so no house to sleep in. Whatever Rah-bee's decision was, right or wrong, it was enforced without the slightest hesitation, with the exception of Prince Ben Daveed (my cousin). The young prince and I would talk when he came back from missions, and he would express his disappointment in certain things being done in the nation; knowing him, I'm sure he stood on that and said his piece no matter the feelings or consequence. That was him. During our childhood, we called him Jabo because he was never afraid to give a punch or take one. And I didn't just take things at face value. It had to make sense, and I had to see the logic at this point; a lot of things had me pondering.

Most of the people really believed that he Rah-bee was the image of God in the flesh and embodied the mystique of God. There was the time that we had begun going to the American Embassy in Tel Aviv to renounce our American citizenship in order to stalemate Israel with the continuous deportations. We had been successful with many, but one day, we all boarded the buses en route to Tel Aviv and were intercepted by Israeli police and were detained until the embassy would close. Now Rah-bee was with us as they herded us into sort of a coral. When they were ready to release us, he wasn't there. There were a lot of us and everyone was busy thinking and trying to analyze our situation and trying to see what they were going to do with us. No one saw him leave, not even me. So what happened to him?

When we boarded the buses for home, he wasn't with us. But when we got to the village, he was there. Everyone was in awe. But there was a brother who was his personal driver, and he drove him to Tel Aviv. The brother wasn't in the coral with us. So I'd say he waited outside and simply drove Rah-bee back to the village, but people denied it saying the driver was in with us too. They wanted to believe that Rah-bee really disappeared and reappeared at the village; there was no refuting what they said they saw and what they just knew was true. Then there was the time when we held a mountainside meeting. It was a special holy meeting of dedication to the spirit. We all left our homes walking to the mountain seeing Rah-bee entering his house not dressed in white as everyone was for the meeting. After we had all been seated, Shaleeak was about to open the meeting when he said, "Behold..." We all turned and saw Rah-bee coming down a steep mountainside, as if he had just miraculously appeared on the mountain. He did walk back with the princes to the village. Yet he would show another side of himself that served to show that he was also humble and one with the people getting involved in various activities just as we did. But even then, sometimes, the people just wouldn't see it.

There once was a basketball game. He played on one of the teams. Basketball being a rough contact sport, there sometimes are injuries. That's a normal thing. But one time, when he played, he was accidentally kicked on the leg. He limped from the game surrounded by all the princes and ministers. The next day, we all learned that his leg had swollen and had some discoloration. The skin had been broken and bled. A decree was sent out that all sneakers were to be collected up and checked out to see which shoe had been the cause of his injury. It was discovered who wore the shoes and what brand they were. We were informed that the brothers were no longer able to use that brand of shoe again. The brother wasn't punished. In the past, I had seen others punished for various offenses. They were chastised and banished for a time determined by him.

In the midst of all of this, we were told, one day, that the Israeli army may be moving in on us to possibly physically remove us from the land. Rah-bee was devising a plan of escape before this would happen. So he sent for three brothers; I was among them. It was on a Saturday. The mission was to be able to get out of Dimona to another city without being detected. Friday sundown to Saturday sundown was our Sabbath. On the Sabbath, we fasted from food and water. But this time, we were going to walk through the mountains. So we each took a pack of dates and a canteen of water. Our destination was the city of Arad. We walked, rested, ate a date or two, drank, and continued on until we reached Arad at sunset Saturday.

When we got to Arad, we were fed a meal, rested, and one of our trucks were waiting to drive us back to Dimona. When we got back, we reported to Rah-bee. Now he knew that it was possible to travel between our cities and maybe through the whole land without being seen except by plane or helicopter. The army never came, and there was no trouble. He was content that it could be done. Everything went on as normal but with Rah-bee becoming more and more elevated to the stature of his holiness. There was a decree sent out forbidding single or married brothers from entertaining single or married sisters behind closed doors even if there was business between you both. However, it was different for him.

There was an order to getting in to see him. You would sit outside on a low wall in front of the rock. One of his wives would come out about 9:00 a.m.—the time he would be ready to have an audience with anyone. Then she would call someone by name to come in. There also would be sisters waiting to see him also. However, the princes, ministers, and deputy ministers could go in ahead of everyone else. If there was room inside the waiting area in the house, you didn't have to wait for someone to come out before you went in. His bedroom was like his office. Many times, I would wait inside to see him, and a sister would come out from behind the closed door of his bedroom. But it was forbidden for the brothers and sisters to do this. At times, he has sent for one of my wives late at night to see them. Once at night, I had occasion to have to talk to him, and while waiting, a sister came out, and I saw that he had a red light on. What could he read, write, or see in a red-light lit room?

Now who would say anything about him not practicing what he had preached? And anyway, who would you say it to? When it came to punishment, no one was exempt, not even the princes. I had never done anything to get on his bad side and needed punishment. He had always exhibited a lot of faith and trust in me—so much so that he would send me out to college campuses and universities to give lecture on his behalf and the plight and purpose of our nation, all in Hebrew. I was the most fluent besides himself and a couple of the princes.

The day came when our band had to travel outside the country to Africa. The band had been led by Prince Keskiyahoo who was, by all rights, an entertainment genius. Now with him away, I was the only other likely person to head the entertainment. We had two bands, the soul messengers and the choice collection. The choice collection remained to perform in Israel along with our gospel choir, dance troupes, and vocal groups. I was the Empresario. Rah-bee agreed to pay me 10 percent of the show's profits. It was workable at first, but the needs of my family grew, and the 10 percent just wasn't enough. Even with my three accounts, I still couldn't keep enough to satisfy my families' needs. So I went to him to ask for a little more to help me. He refused saying I should be glad to get anything he gives me, and there was no way he could see I wasn't able to manage what I had to take care of my family. So I thought, *Here I was representing him all around the country lecturing and actually getting the support of a number of influential Israeli people and boosting the engagements of our entertainment groups because of my acquaintance with a number of entertainment promoters. At times, I would travel to different cities and stay overnight and sometimes a few days to secure contracts for performances for the nation using my own monies until I could get a deposit from a promoter. Even then I would take the entire deposit back to him, still no consideration of additional funds. And here he was controlling everyone's finances and enjoying the benefits of the financial resources of the brothers in the States who were constantly funneling in funds to the nation.* The one who was supposed to be fair and compassionate toward his people had certainly shown me where I stood with him and what I had to do now.

So as it was, as far as pricing the performances and considering the distance that had to be traveled to get to our destination, gas, etc., he would always ask my opinion on this. So I thought I would devise a price list which would include everything. But there would be two price lists, one for him and another one for me. Mine would be inflated by two hundred to three hundred shekels more than his would read. I didn't see any other way to approach the situation. His decisions were supreme; there was no one who would challenge them.

As I was able to do more and more things for my family, I had thought of a way to help some of the brothers as well as help myself. They would invest with me on the cassette duplicating, and they would receive a return of their investment plus 50 percent profit. All was going well until this one brother let it slip to one of the ministers who also happened to be a band member. And he was one of those who, when it came to Rah-bee, you didn't say or do anything without him sanctioning it first, no exceptions; the minister had revealed what I did with the brothers to Rah-bee, and also, one day, one of the promoters had seen him in Tel Aviv and wanted to book a show for a certain price and told him he couldn't afford the price I had given him. This too got back to Rah-bee. He didn't say anything to me right away. Quite a while later, he sent for me. It was only him and me in his room. He told me what was said and said he had confirmed it. Then he said we would talk about it. But meanwhile, I would not be traveling with the band for the time being.

Then there was a decree sent out that my cousin Prince Ben Daveed had been removed as a prince of the nation and was banished from the nation. So that meant if anyone saw him, they were not to speak to him or acknowledge him and that also meant me and his sister Baht-zion. But I did have occasion to see him one day in Beersheba; I spoke to him and embraced him. He was with his entire family. He told me what had happened between him and Rah-bee and that he and the family were returning to America. He didn't try and influence me to leave with them.

Some weeks later, Rah-bee sent for me. He went back over our first sitting about the monies and everything; when things were gravely serious to him when he spoke to you and was bewildered and uncertain as to what to do about it, he always spoke in a low and solemn tone of voice. He said to me that I was like a son to him, and he respected and trusted me. And that I had really disappointed him. And it troubled him greatly that I had thought so little of him as to commit such an offense. Then he said that I was just like my cousin Bendaveed. With that, he said he wanted me to go home and stay there until he sent for me and that he had to listen to the wind and see how it blows before he judges me.

I said to him I didn't care how the wind blows; I was going to leave the land. He asked me to wait and reconsider. I left and went home. I told my wives and children that I would probably be leaving soon. The wives had heard about it already; that was his way to make sure the women were informed of a brother's violation to him and the nation, being ahead of the brother breaking any news to them first. When I told my wives, Anem and Adeevah felt I had harbored the devil in me and that I should go back to Rah-bee and beg his forgiveness. I think they were afraid I would be physically punished, publicly shamed, and cast out of the nation. Shaveev-yah remained silent. She wasn't a rebellious sister, but she had had a few unpleasant encounters with the sisterhood from time to time because she refused to accept certain nonsense things amid them. She and Anem and

Adeevah got along well as my wives; there was no turmoil or strife among them to my knowledge. None of them ever complained.

Anyhow, I expressed to them that I felt that Rah-bee was wrong, and he needs to carefully consider what he might think to do to me. I remained in my house for about two weeks. Some of the ministers would come and talk to me also; some of the princes to discourage me from leaving citing what an asset I was to the nation and that Rah-bee had hinted that my punishment wouldn't be too severe. I was very close to some of them, and we had always shared a mutual respect. Then the day came for his decision. He sent for me. Normally, when you were awaiting his judgment, he would send one of the princes to you with his decision. He began by saying that he felt what I had done didn't merit too severe of a punishment, but that I must pay for what I did. So my punishment was that I would go to work down at the Dead Sea where salt was being processed and shipped out to factories and warehouse. A lot of the brothers worked there. They were not allowed to talk to me or socialize with me, and I was to turn over my entire wages to him, and he would supply my house with food and see to the needs of my family.

As it turned out, the Arab contractor who hired the brothers ended up making me the boss over them. I spoke some Arabic enough to communicate between the brothers and the other Arabs when, at times, there arose disagreements between them. My doing this gave the contractor more time to be away. I learned the supervising aspect of the job fast, and he even gave me an office. A little hand-built shack. But it was comfortable, air-conditioned, and everything. There were brothers who resented my position and abided by the rule of not speaking to me or socializing with me. But there were those who didn't care and came and sat and talked and had lunch with me. I even started to teach them a little Arabic. At first, the boss would ride to the village with us and turn the checks over to Rah-bee. But now, he had set it up for the brothers to cash their own checks. He had set up an account where the brothers would sign a sheet, and I would take the sheet and checks to the bank and cash them and divide the money among the brothers. The brothers were glad to be able to see their own money before Rah-bee did, then they could see how much he was taking from them each payday. When Rah-bee got word of this, although they still had to turn their money in to him, he was displeased that I was made boss over the brothers, and I was in charge of cashing their checks. So he appointed a minister to come down on payday to collect all the checks each week. There was nothing he could do about me being supervisor, and the brothers having to talk to me. This part of my punishment didn't last too long. I guess he realized I was just a born leader without even trying to be. So now he came up with another idea. He had a snowball cart made, and I was to supply it and sell snowballs at the city marketplace. I'd get up early, push the cart to a specific area around the marketplace, and set up and sell snowballs; he had lifted the ban on me being spoken to by the brothers. That was just for the time at the Dead Sea works. Everyone else in the village was able to talk to me anyway.

I was to sell snowballs, take him the proceeds, and go straight into my house until the next morning. I was still restricted from socializing with the other brothers and sisters. He never had anyone with me to watch and see that I wasn't taking any money. Also, as part of my punishment, I would have to take a shift at standing guard at night as this was already mandatory for all brothers except deputy ministers, ministers, and princes. My shifts were more regular than others; my sleep would be broken many times if another brother wasn't feeling well or had another responsibility to carry out for Rah-bee. I didn't like it. Although I never lost my title as deputy minister, I had no standing as one anymore. Although my punishment wasn't as harsh as some I had witnessed, I still felt it was unfair, and now my manhood was being slowly stripped for my wives and others to see me like this after all my dedicated service to him.

Later, I was told I would be riding to the market at four-thirty or five in the morning with the brothers who made market for the village once or twice a week. But that I would now be selling watermelons and grapes at another market site not far outside the village, and I'd have to get out there before sunrise to secure a spot each morning. Even with this, I still had security duty each night. The more these things took place, the stronger my feelings got that I not only wanted to leave but had too because I wasn't going to take much more. And knowing myself, it would be better for all involved.

Then one day, Rah-bee sent for me. When I got there, my cousin Baht-zion was also there. As we sat in the waiting area inside his house, we both were surprised that each of us was there. Neither of us had a clue. He asked us both to come into his room. When we sat down, he told us that Bendaveed had come back to Israel. And he had wanted to see us. He said there were no hard feeling between them and Baht-zion, and I could go up to see him. So we did. He and one of his wives M'sha-vee-elah were at the Sheraton hotel in Tel Aviv. We were all glad to see each other. He had returned not to rejoin the nation but to see Baht-zion and I and see how we were doing.

Also, he had returned to do business with a company that extracted sea salt from the Dead Sea. He had planned to package it and import it to the States. We sat and talked awhile. Baht-zion and I knew the details of his leaving the nation. So we didn't get into that so much. The conversation mainly centered around how the family was doing and the progress he and M'sha-vee-elah had made in various ventures in the States. He never once tried to convince us that we should leave Israel. Later that evening, we all went out to a nice vegetarian restaurant to eat. We all went back to the hotel and sat awhile together. Then Baht-zion and I returned to the village. I told my family how well they were looking and doing for themselves. Knowing that I was thinking of leaving Israel, none of the wives expressed a desire to follow me.

It was customary on the Sabbath (Saturday) for brothers, sisters, and children to go for walks in the park, sit, and study or just relax. This one Sabbath, Anim and Adeevah didn't feel like going, so I and Sha-vee-v-yah went alone. We lay our blanket on the grass and held hands. Sha-veev-yah asked me if I was really going to leave. I told her yes, and that I wasn't going to ask her or Anim and Adee-vah to leave with me nor was I going to try and take my and Anim's children with me. Because I had been gone from America for fifteen years now, I didn't know what would be in store for me when I return, so

I wouldn't subject my children to it. And they're all that Anim has, and I wouldn't do that to her.

Then Shaveevyah said to me that she too wanted to leave and take Ohay-vee-yah with her. So we made plans to leave. Some of the ministers and princes continued to come by and sit and talk with me trying to convince me not to leave. Then Rah-bee sent for me again to come see him. I thought maybe he was ready to lift my punishment. As I waited to see him, I kept telling myself no matter what he said or did I was still going to leave. Well, I went in. He said to me that my punishment was over, but he needed me to do something that night. It was Friday night—the Sabbath, which would last until Saturday at sundown. He very seldom had anyone come to him on the Sabbath.

He told me that Ben-daveed had come back to Israel again. And he wanted to know exactly what his purpose and intentions were. He asked if I had any wine at the house. I did. He told me to drink a lot of it so I would reek of it. He wanted me to tell Ben-daveed I was disgruntled and had planned to leave. But I was really going to leave anyway. Maybe he thought the ministers and princes had convinced me not to. I drank as much wine as I could hold. I told the wives what I was doing so they wouldn't think I was being outright defiant. I went the back way from my house so no one else would see me or stop me. I crossed the mountains past the Dimona complex to another building where a sister named Mal-ka lived who had left the nation. When they opened the door, they were surprised to see me on the Sabbath; however, Ben-daveed was especially glad to see me but was reluctant to offer me some of the cocktail he was having. But I agreed to have some with him. Then I told him about why I had come. So together, we devised a false report for Rah-bee along the lines that he had come back to get some of the people to leave the nation and follow him. He was starting his own following, and he would be in the land for a while when, in actuality, he had only returned to follow up on his first visit to further the business of the salt importing from the Dead Sea to the States. I returned to the K'far, but it was late, so I waited until morning to report to Rah-bee.

85

When I did report to him, he seemed sort of bewildered and puzzled. He said to me that I did a good job. There were some of the princes sitting outside the door waiting to see him. As I left, he asked me to tell one of the ministers outside to have the rest of the princes come over. I sensed they were going to meet about Ben-daveed's presence in the land and his intentions. Not long after, Ben-daveed left to go back. I wouldn't be far behind.

The time came for Shaveev-yah and I to leave. I had never intended to take my children, but Shaveev-yah was going to take Ohay-vee-yah, her daughter. It was no secret we were leaving, and as it was Rah-bee's way, he never would allow anyone leaving the nation to take their children with them, and Israel's government wouldn't interfere. He had Shaveev-yah's daughter sent to another city, out of reach. I assured Shaveev-yah that I would find a way to get her out. We left one evening. My boys, Ben-Shamoor, Shmu-el, and Yakeen, followed us crying and holding on to me begging me to take them with me. They followed all the way to the bus station. I kissed and embraced them all together in a big hug, and I cried with them and told them to go back to their mom. That she would hurt and miss them if they left her. They stood there until the bus pulled away crying loudly. All the passengers were looking out at them saying in Hebrew, "Poor little ones," and they glanced at me and Shaveev-yah with a question mark expression.

We continued on to Tel Aviv. I had known some Israeli's who owned a hotel called Hotel Eilat. I had a little money on me that would hold us for a few days. Also, I knew that the embassy would help Shaveev-yah because she was still as US citizen. When she had come to Israel, the deportations had stopped, and we had ended the renunciation of our citizenship. The embassy would pay for her to stay in the hotel and give her money for food. And my friends would let me stay even if I had no funds. Meanwhile, we stayed at the Eilat Hotel. And we both had been to the embassy to get the process started to be able to get back to the States. They explained that mine would be lengthy because I had renounced my citizenship. So we made the best of our situation. We took in the sites during the day enjoying some of the venues in the evening and just spending all of our time with each other. I dreaded the day coming when she would be leaving me behind. But I reassured her that I would figure a way to get Ohay-vee-yah out before I left. There were others living in Tel Aviv that had left the nation. Sometimes, we would go and visit with them. Then the day came that Shaveev-yah would be leaving.

I rode to the airport with her and saw her board the plane. On my way back to the hotel, I looked out of the window of the taxi, checked my watch, and looked up to see the flight she'd be on ascending into the night sky. It was a very lonely feeling. But I had to remain strong, focused, and vigilant as to where I would go from there. I remained at the hotel for another few months or so, then I would stay at youth hostels around the Jerusalem area. My funds were really low. I had very little left in my bank accounts.

Then one day, I met a reporter who remembered me from when I was traveling with the band. She said she had seen a performance and I wasn't in it so she asked about me, and they told her that I had left the band and the community. She began to ask me about it, and she started writing articles on my leaving the community and my views on what I felt was reason enough for me to leave after all those years.

After that, I found myself doing a lot of interviews and lectures that I was compensated for. There were always articles in the newspapers, and at some point, I did a couple of radio programs. This wasn't aimed at degrading Rah-bee and the community or me trying to get others to leave. It was only about me. But certain reports fabricated my words and intentions. One radio station wanted the public to hear my side and Rah-bee's side at the same time on the air. The station set up an interview with Rah-bee without him knowing I would be there. When he came to the station and saw me there, he refused to go on with the interview. This too was broadcast to the public. I was still thinking of ways to get Shaveev-yah's daughter away from the nation. Because for some reason, I was told by the American embassy that they could not intervene, and I would need power of attorney to expedite that.

Meanwhile, I had devised a plan to kidnap her. I had gotten two of my Israeli friends to dress in Arab headdress, and so was I; sitting low in the rear seat of a car, we drove to the village to where the children were playing, and I attempted to call her over, but one of the other children felt something wasn't right and ran to tell the brothers. So we left; I didn't try again. In the meantime, I kept checking with the embassy on my status every other week with no word yet. Now I, at least, wanted to see my children once more before I left the country. So I decided to go down to the K'far knowing Rah-bee and many of the others would be angry and shun me, but I didn't care. I wanted to see my children, not just my biological children but all of them. So I arrived at the village to be met by some of the brothers. They told me they had orders not to let me into the village. I told them I just wanted to see my children and that I would stay outside the entrance, and they could bring them to the stairs. They refused. So I went to the police station and talked to a policeman name Soli. He was familiar with the nation and Rah-bee's rule over the people. So he returned with me. And he convinced Rah-bee to allow me to see them. But I was not allowed to enter the house; instead, it was arranged for me to meet with them and the wives at the nation's banquet hall. I entered first, then they all came. My children ran to me with hugs.

I explained why I had left and about things that had taken place since I've been out of the nation. The conversation was very cordial and non-argumentative. I told my children why I wasn't going to try and take them away from their mom and told them when they were of age, they would make their own decision. And that if they came to the States, they would find me. Soli and I left. He asked where I was staying in Jerusalem so he could keep in touch and just in case I needed his help. Soli knew me from coming to the station many times when some of the brothers and younger men would get into little situations, and Rah-bee would send me to get the report and what was happening with them. And even sometimes going to court to translate from Hebrew to them exactly what was going on. Then he told me of a friend of his who worked for the housing authority in case I needed somewhere to stay other than at the youth hostels. We exchanged information and I left.

Then one day, as I was walking through Jerusalem, I met a brother who had left the nation long before me; his Hebrew name was Ah-mee-el, and his birth name was Charles. Charles had grown up with Ben-daveed and I and several others who came to Israel when Ben-daveed first came. Ah-mee-el was living with a Jewish young lady there in Jerusalem, and he offered me to come and stay with them. I would be great company for him, and he for me. The young lady was very nice and respectable. As I stayed there, Ah-mee-el and I mostly sat around and talked during the day. The young lady worked during the day. We all got along real good. I would contribute to the groceries each week.

I would travel to Tel Aviv from time to time to check on my status of returning to the States. The last visit, they were waiting on documents they had sent to my grandmother and my father to come back for them to forward to Washington for approval.

Later, I noticed that, sometimes, Ah-mee-el would want to go out very early in the day and stay out 'til late in the evening. Then I finally learned that her parents had come to Israel to visit and check up on her. And they had rented the apartment for her and Ah-mee-el couldn't be seen there when they came. They didn't know about them. And if they found out, they would take away the apartment and take her back to the States. This went on for a while until I decided to check with Soli's friend from the housing authority.

So one day, I traveled to Arad to see this friend. His name was Amit. When I arrived at his apartment, I introduced myself. Soli had already sent word to him that I might be getting in touch. They were a very nice and receptive family. That very day, I was made totally welcome. Amit took me around the neighborhood, and he introduced me to all the neighbors and a group of his personal friends. When we returned, his wife had prepared me a place to sleep, and pajamas were laid out. She had selected me a washcloth, bath towel, and toothbrush. There were even a pair of house shoes for me. I was given the privilege of going into the refrigerator whenever I wanted and come and go as I pleased.

Then one day, after Amit and I had had several conversations about why I left the nation and my situation with the embassy, he asked me to go with him to Jerusalem to an important business dinner. There were some important people he wanted me to meet, and he was sure they would be glad to meet me. I had a nice powder blue suit to wear and a hat. Amit thought it would be a nice touch to have a briefcase as some of them would carry one. I had no idea who these people were going to be. We entered this fine restaurant and were shown to a table where three well-dressed gentlemen were seated. Small amounts of papers sprawled here and there. They were talking away in Hebrew. I understood everything they were saying. Then Amit introduced me. They each stood and shook my hand. They were David Glass of the national religious party, Yosef Burg, the interior minister, and Jaque Amir, the mayor or Dimona. They were interested in knowing about the roots of the community, the structure, and motivation of the existence and persistence of the people, what influenced me to become a part of it, and what, after years of representing the community throughout Israel, prompted me to part ways. They, in turn, shared their views and opinions of Rah-bee and ideas of solving the so-called problem of "the Black Hebrews."

The things I heard were not of a negative tone at all. They explained Israel's position in regards to me and the American embassy and Washington. They each personally agreed to do what they could to help in my return to the States. Also, at that meeting, I learned from the mayor of Dimona and Amit who worked for the Israeli Housing Authority that the nation still had a few rent-free years to go. And that if Rah-bee was already collecting rent, it wasn't by their request or demand, and no rent was being received from him. Well, after our exchange, dinner was served. As I searched the menu, it was hard to decide. So Amit, sitting next to me, when he was served had some unusual but tasty looking meatball-like things on his plate. He gave me a taste. It was delicious with a nice sauce and all, so I told the waiter I would have the same. When they brought my plate to me, I couldn't wait to dig in. Yum! When I had finished the whole plate, I asked Amit what that was. He said in Hebrew, "Bayt-say-shore" (bull's eggs). Literally, bull's testicles. We all laughed, and I said, "My first meat in fifteen years, and this had to be it!" The dinner ended, and Amit and I drove back to his house. The next day, Amit told me he would do all he could to help me with the embassy holdup and see about finding some legal loopholes to help get Ohayvee-yah out.

Amit worked feverishly at it for the next few months but to no avail. Soon, I received the power of attorney from Sha-veev-yah in the States, but it held no weight in Israel. I decided I would just wait until I got to the States to try and help Shaveev-yah get her daughter out. Meanwhile, it seemed the embassy wasn't doing enough to help me. So I decided to call my sister Barbara to check on what progress my grandma and dad was making about getting the documents and info the embassy needed to forward to Washington. I tried to call my sister as least as possible because I always had to call collect. Given the time difference, when it was one or two o'clock in the afternoon in Israel, it was ten or eleven o'clock at night in the States. But no matter the hour, Barbara never refused to take my calls. She kept me up-to-date on what progress was being made. Also, while I had been gone, my brothers James and Edward had passed away and also my sister Maryann.

Well, things did brighten up a little. While in Jerusalem, one day I, met a Jewish rabbi named Golding. He had been following the Black Hebrew situation in Israel and had heard a lot about me. We would meet a few times and talk, sort of feeling each other out and getting to know each other. Then one day, he said he had a house in Yerokam not far from Jerusalem that he and the family wasn't using and that I could live there rent free until I left Israel.

I immediately took him up on his offer. Rabbi Golding was a well-known rabbi throughout Israel. He had achieved a considerable reputation for his anti-missionary work against cults and sects of any kind. He drove me to the house in Yerokam. It was late at night when we entered; he showed me through the house which was at ground level with a nice kitchen, bath, and shower, a spacious living room, a garden porch, and a linen closet full of bedding. There were two nice-sized bedrooms. Lights and gas were on. And there was a telephone.

Rabbi Golding went out and bought food to stock the refrigerator and the cabinets. He ate kosher, and I was a vegetarian, so the shopping list was very agreeable. Rabbi told me the utilities were paid for six months in advance. This is the way he always did. It wasn't specially for me. He said that I could use the telephone all I want and also to make calls back to the states. He left, and I never saw or heard from him again.

Then one day, in my travels, I ran across Amiel again. He came and stayed a few days. Then one day, a knock came at the door, and there stood two sisters he and I knew along with their children. They had left the nation. There was plenty of room, so I invited them to stay at the house as long as I would be there because I would be leaving for the States, hopefully within the near future. They all stayed. Amiel and I took the sisters out dancing and socializing throughout the Yerokam community. We all were well-received by all the neighbors. Well, it appeared that the sisters just needed a break and time to decide what they really wanted to do. After about two weeks, they decided they would return to the village. Later, Amiel left and returned to Jerusalem. I enjoyed the company but didn't mind the solitude. My main focus was on that day when I would get the news that I would be leaving Israel.

Meanwhile, I met an Israeli named Haim Chertok. He was a writer for one of the Israeli newspapers. He lived right there in Yerokam; we had a very nice encounter. He asked if he could interview me and wanted to do a series of articles on me. I agreed, and we began to meet from time to time, sometimes at his home and sometimes at mine. I felt the friendship and interviews were very fruitful. He had a very nice family and made me welcome all the time. Sometimes, it was just socially.

Then one day, when I traveled to Jerusalem, I ran into some of the brothers who had also left the nation. I was invited to visit them in Jerusalem. One day, I did. I was surprised at what I found when I showed up at the address they had given me. It was a partially abandoned apartment building. They had no electricity or water except a lot of water cooler jugs of water all around. They slept on blankets on the floor and a couple of run-down couches. And they were into lots of drinking hard liquor and a drug called Hashish. They smoked. I drank wine and did pick up smoking cigarettes, but my pride and dignity wouldn't let me sink to that level just because I was no longer a part of the nation and could do what I want. After that visit, I never went again. But I would see them from time to time in passing.

Then I ran into Amiel again. He told me about some guy who had some special document that he had that helps people who can't get passports get out of countries to wherever they want to go. He had examples of the documents—letters supposedly from people who actually used his document. He even had rubber stamps that he compared with photocopies of actual foreign government stamps. He called it the international passport. It had a really official look to it. He wanted passport photos and application fees, the whole works. I knew better, and I was surprised that Amiel had been taken by that. I wanted out of Israel, true enough, but not foolish enough and too impatient not to endure and wait for the embassy to get results.

As time passed, I met Roberta, a newspaper journalist. She too was very interested in the story of my life with the Black Hebrews of Dimona. We had many meetings, lunches, and dinners, and we began to spend some leisure time together. Then it became evident that the relationship was turning personal. We began to see each other more regularly and call and talk more often and more personal. I was reluctant at first because of the wives I'd left behind. But the reality was that they were going to stay in Israel and the tradition was that after a husband or wife leaves the nation, the husband or wife that is left after a brief period can remarry. So knowing this, I pursued what was transforming between Roberta and me with all seriousness. We began dating even though I'd be leaving sometime soon and she would more than likely remain in Israel. She wondered, and so did I. *How would we continue this once I left, and how would it be if she came to the States to be with me? How would that go with Sha-veev-yah?*

Then one day, Roberta told me that she would be going to the States in the near future. And if I'm gone before she does, she'll be coming to find me. So we both exchanged addresses where we could find each other in the States. After hearing nothing positive from the embassy for nearly a year, I arrived home one afternoon and checked the mail as usual, not expecting to find anything from the embassy. Then it happened. Finally, an answer from Washington and an appointment to come to the embassy to get my travel papers, and I'd be leaving in one month. I did get to say one last goodbye to the wives and children and to Roberta and most of the friends I had made while in Jerusalem and Tel Aviv. I called my sister Barbara and my cousin Ben-daveed to let them know when I would be leaving. But it was strange that the embassy would only get me to New York. I'd have to make my way the rest of the way on my own. I told Ben-daveed about this, and he arranged to have a ticket sent ahead to New York to help me get to Chicago. One thing that I could always be sure of is that I could always count on him to come through when I needed him.

Finally, I'm on my way. The plane stops over in Frankfurt, Germany. Everyone is told that, in the meantime, they could go out to some shops, etc. for a designated time and had to be back in time to take their connecting flight to New York. Everyone began leaving past the gate showing their documents. When I approached the gate, there was a delay as the officials were speaking in German and looking at my papers. Then another official was called over and then came to me and explained in English that I could not leave the airport because the document I had was a non-citizen travel document, not a passport, and so I could not leave the airport until it was time to board my flight to New York. It was a few hours. So I tried to get as comfortable as possible. I wouldn't nap or sleep for fear I would be left. Then what would I do?

I had learned a little German while in Israel but not enough to help me in this situation. Well, it was time to leave. There were no problems boarding to New York. When I arrived, my ticket to Chicago was there as David had promised. I landed at O'Hare Airport. David and Maxine (M'sha-vee-elah), his wife, were waiting. I got a few strange looks from a few people in the airport. I couldn't figure why? We drove down one of the city streets of the west side. Things looked quite different (the clothes, cars, and buildings) from what I remembered when I left in 1971. It was now 1984. It was another time zone. Later, when we arrived at the house, David said, "Cous, you're going to need a whole new wardrobe. These clothes have to go. And that suitcase is like something from the twenties."

We all laughed; I felt like a refugee. We settled in. I wanted to smoke. David and Maxine didn't smoke, but allowed me to go out to their rear porch to smoke. I never thought I would be relieved to smell the smoggy and polluted air of America again. The phone rang, and David came out to get me. It was my sister Barbara and my cousin Hermatte. They were eager to see me. David had prepared a spare bedroom for me, so I told Barbara and Hermatte I would see them the next day. They wouldn't have it. They were going to take a taxi that night. David lived in forest park, and they were on the south side of Chicago, quite a distance to take a taxi. They came, and we laughed, talked, and cried some together. They left, and we retired for the night.

The next day, David would show me how to take the public transportation to the south side. He explained the fare system to me, but he neglected to tell me that the buses didn't give change anymore. I had exact change from Forest Park to the south side, but when I boarded the bus on the south side to get to Barbara's house, I put a $5 bill into the money box and stood there waiting for my change. After a minute or two, the driver asked what was I waiting for? I said my change. He pointed to the sign on the box that said exact change. There was nothing he could do about it, so this was my first reality check, so to speak.

Being unfamiliar with the system, I should have asked. I took it as a lesson of look before you leap! I made it to Barbara's house, and it was a real warm welcome. Cousins came from everywhere; it seemed like once things settled down, I was going to be staying at Barbara's. Family continued to come by and welcome me home. Shaveevyah (Doris) came and spent a couple of days with me. Then the family arranged a welcome home get together for me at the Grand Ballroom on Sixty-Fourth and Cottage Grove. It was all sheer bliss.

David drove me around to see other family. My dad would drive me around through the old neighborhood and places pointing out the change in things and people. It was quite an experience. For about the first couple of months, my sister Barbara and her husband Robert went to work each day, and I'd just stay home and relax. Barbara would give me money each payday. I very seldom went out, so the money would just accumulate more and more. Barbara never once asked me to look for work or look for a place of my own. But I knew it was time I did those things.

Me with no background, references, or certain job-required skills, it was difficult to get something right away, so Barbara told me about the general assistance program. That would give me a monthly check and food stamps. When I would receive them each month, Barbara never accepted anything, but instead had me to keep it for myself. She never asked of me to pay anything for staying with her and Robert. At first, I was always being driven around everywhere. But then one day, Robert rented a car. I had gotten my driver's license. So I wanted to borrow the car to go out and visit with family. Robert let me borrow the car. I wanted to also go to some of the old neighborhoods and look up some very old friends.

David had wanted me to stay in Forest Park with him and Maxine when I came, but I was eager to get back to the South side. He had told me that things and people we had known weren't the same, and the drug game had taken them over. I felt I could handle it. So I drove down to Thirty-Fifth and State Street to the Stateway Gardens where we used to hang out years ago. I was sure to run into some of the guys we had known, and it wouldn't be so bad once they remembered me, I thought. I pulled up in the rental car—a Chrysler LeBaron, white with all white interior. I wore a suit and tie with a nice hat, and I had on a gold bracelet and a small diamond ring on. I saw a group of guys; they approached the car. I recognized them, and they recognized me. I asked where a couple of my cousins lived who used to be around the area back then.

They said that they lived on Thirty-Ninth and State Street. They got in the car to show me exactly where. There were three of them. One of them sat in front with me, and the other two sat in back. We laughed and talked of the old times. We pulled into the parking lot of the building where they said my cousins lived. Then all of a sudden, I was grabbed from behind around my throat. Then the one beside me hit me in the eye and mouth. I could vaguely see a gun. I didn't feel anything because I was angry that these guys who I knew were doing this to me. They wrestled me out of the car; I was still struggling and cursing. They told me to stop struggling and shut up and that they didn't want to hurt me. They took my jewelry and my shoes and threw me on the floor in the back. Two of them sat in the back and had their feet out on me. I could hardly see. But I was able to see the streetlights and parts of the buildings from my position. Then I could tell which direction they were taking me. All of a sudden, the car stopped. The one driving got out. He asked the others what liquor they wanted and had the nerve to ask me too from the money they had taken from me. He came back, and they drove off. I could tell they were driving toward the Dan Ryan Expressway. I didn't think I would live through it—the way they were driving on the expressway. Then they began throwing out all of my identification; they called it out as they tossed it. Then they pulled over off the expressway and dragged me out of the car and pulled off. I stood up blind in one eye and with a blurry vision in the other, bloodied, and barefoot. I had lost my direction for a second, But then I sensed which way was south.

I stood there for a moment hoping someone would pull over since the traffic that night wasn't very heavy. No one did. And I know they could see me clearly in their headlights. So I began to walk. I got off the expressway by walking up the ramp at Forty-Third Street. I went to a gas station to ask for help. The attendant refused saying he didn't want to be involved. He wouldn't even call the police. I stood outside near the gas pumps as people pulled in, got gas, and just pulled away. No one asked if I needed help, but later, a taxi pulled in; the driver was Hispanic or Arab. He asked if I needed help. I told him my story. He had me to sit in the cab while he went in for cigarettes. I told him where I needed to go but had no money and that he would be paid when I got there. I was more worried how Barbara and Robert would react to me losing the car than I was about myself as I was more angry and disappointed at myself for not listening to David and using common sense. So Robert and Barbara got me to the hospital. I was checked out and released. The next couple of weeks, I stayed in and recuperated. Doris came by and helped to nurse me back to health for a few days.

Then I began to focus on getting her daughter Ohay-vee-yah (Sharon) back to her from Israel. So I arranged a meeting with Rahbee's representative Prince Ah-see-el who acted as the ambassador for the nation. I had a meeting with him at the McCormick place.

During our meeting, he realized that not accommodating me could prove more harmful than helpful for him and the nation in no uncertain terms. We came to a mutual agreement that he would get word to Rah-bee in Israel as to what needs to be done in returning Doris's daughter to her as soon as possible. This made Doris very happy to know that she soon would be reunited with her daughter.

As time went on, I decided to move from Barbara's house to a place of my own. So as I searched, I found a room on Sixty-Fourth and Parnell. This was ideal because Doris lived on Sixty-Ninth and Parnell, and now I could be closer to her, and maybe soon, we'd find a place together. We visited back and forth with each other and talked of getting a place together. But as time went on, somehow, we became more and more distant. Her visits with me became less and less. And when I would call, she seemed to never be home. So it sort of just fizzled out between us. Our marriage in Israel wasn't legally binding or recognized in the States, so we each went our separate ways.

During this time, I never knew whether her daughter was returned or not. And I had no further dealings with Ah-see-el or the nation. I eventually moved from my room on Parnell after I had been bitten by a rat. The building was inspected and found the basement to be infested. I pursued the issue, but nothing ever came of it. So I learned that Grandma Joanna who I hadn't seen since I had gotten back was living at Fifty-Sixth and Sangamon, not too far from where I lived. I called and spoke to my cousin Hermatte who was now caring for her, my brother Howard, and cousin Lavance. Hermatte offered me to come and live with them. It was really good to see Grandma again. By now, she had lost both her legs. But she was still as outspoken as ever and still had a little fire left in her. It was quite a reunion.

Then one day, as I was sitting upstairs, I heard a lot of strange voices and people coming up the stairs. I saw a sort of spotlight beaming into the room. To my surprise, Roberta came in from Israel with a camera crew. She had found me just like she said she would. She interviewed me about my trip home and any experiences I had after I got back and my plans now that I was back. We walked out and talked about us and where we stood as far as what had transpired between us in Israel. She was going to be living in a distant city, and I wasn't ready to leave my family, so we decided amicably to just stay in touch and visit when we could. We continued to write to each other. Then one day, we just lost touch.

Then one day, I met with David, and he was selling a car that his dad had left to him. He and Maxine were buying another car. This was a great opportunity for me to be able to get around independently and help Hermatte getting Grandma to and from the hospital. And it would make it easier for me to get around while looking for jobs. While the job hunting wasn't going too well, I still had to make appointments at the public aid office in order to keep getting assistance from them.

Then one day, as I went to one appointment while waiting for my name to be called, I heard the name "Dwight Banks." I wondered if this could be the same Dwight Banks that I knew who had grown up at Thirty-Fifth Street with us and used to hang out at the Black Box; we used to ride out to his grandmother's house in Harvey with our girlfriends. He also had that cute little sister Michelle who was four years younger than me, and he wouldn't think about seeing me bothering her. But I always said that I was going to get her one day. After the name was called, I looked up to see who would answer to it. And to my surprise, it was the Dwight Banks I knew. Luckily, they didn't call me until he had finished. I approached him, and it was a happy reunion. I asked him to wait for me. I drove him home. He reintroduced me to the family. We were all mostly young when I left. I asked where Michelle was; Dwight said she'd be coming over on Mother's Day, so I made plans to definitely be there on that day.

Dwight called me on Mother's Day and said Michelle was there, and he hadn't told her I was coming. When I got there, there was a house full of people. As I looked around, I spotted her. Dwight called her over and asked if she knew who I was. She paused for a few minutes, but then she recognized me. We sat on the porch and talked about when we were young. She remembered how I teased about getting her one day. She said, "So you're still trying?" Then she called over a young man and introduced him as her son; his name was

James. Maybe he was about eleven or twelve years old. Afterward, Michelle asked if I would take her and James home. I agreed. We sat and talked until daybreak.

From then on, we began seeing each other regularly. After a while, we moved in together. I still didn't have a job at this time. But that didn't matter to Michelle; whatever we had, we shared. Michelle was working as a security officer at Powell School in the South Shore area. We were doing well and very happy. I stayed home and did some cooking while she worked. Things worked out well between us.

Then suddenly, one day, the news came that my father had passed. It was the first and hardest lost I had suffered since my return. My cousin Marvin was a daily pillar of strength for me through that time. Eventually, Michelle and I had to move. So we were offered to come and live with Grandma and Hermatte at Seventy-Ninth and Drexel with my brother Howard and cousin Lavance who Hermatte was caring for. I would help out with them while Michelle would help care for Grandma who now was a double amputee. Hermatte later moved out, and Michelle and I remained.

With all that's needed to be done each day, we still had time for our social enjoyments. Then once again, tragedy would strike. This time, it was literally very close to home. Lavance had a history of seizures and normally would bounce back from them. But this one time, he didn't make it. We would miss his energy and entertaining personality. Not long after, Grandma got sick and was hospitalized. She remained in the hospital for quite a while.

In the meantime, the landlord was selling the building, and the new owners wanted the old tenants out. So Michelle and James moved to one of Michelle's sister's house, just when we were about to be able to save and get a place of our own. Well, James and Michelle would be staying at Michelle's sister's house and I would stay at the apartment as long as I could and then maybe find a room to rent somewhere until we could be together again and hopefully in our own apartment. I had about a month or so to stay there.

I contacted David and explained the situation to him. He had started an import/export business in the Oak Park suburb. He hired me to work in his office. I did rent a room on the south side.

Michelle came and lived there with me while James lived with one of his aunts. Well, this lasted for quite a few months until the building started falling into disrepair, and there was a rodent problem. Once again, we hadn't saved for an apartment. So it was time to move, and we would be separated again. But I still would stay there until I had found somewhere to move.

Then one day, while David and I were out of the office in a downtown restaurant pub called Millers—having a few cocktails as we occasionally did after a good day at the office—I met a young lady. We had a few cocktails and got acquainted with each other. We decided to leave together. We left David and took the train to the south side to get my car so I could drive her in the Roseland area—the 100s. Her name was Sandra. She lived with her mom, her two small daughters and her brother. I liked her, but I was with Michelle.

Then one day, when Michelle came home, I forgot about what, but we had a heated argument. It resulted in Michelle leaving and me not being able to reach her at her job as I normally did. And I wouldn't go by any of her family's houses, so I felt that she had gone for good. So I continued to see Sandra and later moved out of my room and in with her and her two daughters and her mom. I continued to work with David. I hadn't heard anything from Michelle for quite some time. Later, Sandra and I moved in together, and we moved into our own apartment on Seventy-Third and Loomis.

I still couldn't get Michelle out of my system remembering how dedicated and supportive she had been to me through everything. So I finally made contact with her at her job. I told her I had moved in with Sandra. It hurt her bad; she cried as we talked and I felt sick. But it was done. There were no problems between Sandra and me, but I still just had to see Michelle. I continued to see and be with her from time to time.

Sandra became suspicious of my coming in later and later. And one day, we got into a heated argument, and I raised my hand to strike Sandra but I didn't. She just stood and stared at me then went into the bedroom and locked the door. She had told me how abusive the children's father had been to her. And I had promised that I would never do that to her.

The next morning, she came out with bags packed and said she loved me, but she thought we needed some time apart to sort things out and that she and the girls would be going back to her mother's. I would go by and visit with her, and once in a while spend the night. But nothing was certain about her returning home to me. She would come by and spend time with me from time to time, but I knew we were done. We had not been together for even a year. I still lived at the apartment. Sandra stopped coming by, and we didn't communicate much anymore. We sort of just drifted apart. There was no discussion of reuniting.

I got in touch with Michelle. And she came and stayed with me in the apartment. Then she called me one day and said there had been a fire in the building. I rushed home to find firetrucks everywhere. The stairway was burned and wet from the water hoses. Michelle was outside scared and shaken up. After a while, we were allowed back into the building. It was a mess inside the apartment. All the windows were broken out and some parts of the walls. Michelle and I still stayed there for another week or two. Once again, Michelle went back to her sister's house, and I ended up staying in another office that David had rented in the same building.

The owner, an Italian gentleman named Sam Ciccio, came one day and discovered I was staying there. He had met me before and actually hired me to paint one of the bathrooms in the building. He liked David, so he didn't make a fuss about it. Later, I brought Michelle out to spend a few days with me. David was aware of it and allowed us to be there until he would be ready to furnish it and open for business. Michelle and I would even cook there.

One day, the landlord came by and smelled our cooking and complimented how good it smelled but just warned us of cooking during the day when other tenants were in their offices. Then Sam asked if I wouldn't mind doing a few odd jobs around the building from time to time with pay. I agreed. He showed me all there was to be done on a regular basis. David never opened the second office and eventually gave up the first one. I remained working for Sam. He eventually rented out the office that I was staying in. So I went with

Michelle to stay at her sister's on the south side. But I would travel to Oak Park to work for Sam.

I finally got the sense to open a bank account and start saving money. Michelle and I eventually left her sister's and rented a room on Forty-Seventh Street on the south side. Soon after, we found a three-room apartment across the street from where we lived. The bathroom was down the hall, but we did have a kitchen, bedroom, and living room. We hadn't had that much living space together since Michelle's apartment.

Then one day, to my utmost surprise as I was sitting out on the back porch, I looked up, and there was Samuel, my next to the oldest son. It was truly a dream come true. There wasn't a day that passed by that I hadn't longed to have my children with me. But I knew it would be better if they were of age to make a sound decision themselves. We spent most of that day together reminiscing over the times in Israel and sharing a tear or two both of joy and a little disappointment—the joy of seeing each other after all these years and me living in the neighborhood I did and not living in houses and places like the ones that was projected in films and photos sent back by some who had gone back to the States on mission. But yet Samuel never spoke an ill word just that I could sense it! He wouldn't be able to stay and meet Michelle that time. But it was such an elated feeling to have seen and embraced him. He told me that his brother was planning to come also. I knew that Yeef-ah, being the baby, would still remain in Israel with her mom.

Samuel was living with his aunt Barbara on the south side. Every now and then, I would travel to spend time with him. We had such good times. It was a good season for me and for Samuel as Barbara's intended husband Robert had three sons and two daughters. Samuel began dating one of the daughters (Tasha); they eventually got married and blessed me with two beautiful grandsons who they named Korey and Kasey. Now Barbara and Robert had gotten married. So now, I had nieces and nephews: Shawn, Derrick, Laronne, Tonya, and Tasha. Tasha would have a dual title, niece and also daughter in law! I felt really blessed. If that wasn't enough, my youngest, Yakeen, arrived a few years later. After him, my eldest Ben-shamoor (Melvin

Jr.) came. How great was this? All my sons here where I can talk to and see them when I want, and I had experienced the pros and cons of the new way of life they might encounter. But now they had lots of family to clue them in. Carolyn and I stayed in constant touch in regard to their welfare. I never knew how Doris came out with her daughter.

The building where Michelle and I lived had become a haven for drug dealers and addicts mixed with late-night disturbances. No one bothered us day or night. We became known to just about everyone in the neighborhood including the gang bangers. But there start to appear too many new faces in the building, and the disturbances became louder and more often without police intervention so we thought it best to move.

I got the idea to approach Sam Ciccio about me becoming his live-in maintenance man for the building. For this, he would have to transform part of an office suite into an apartment for me. He agreed. So Michelle again moved to her sisters until it would be ready. It was ready in a couple of months. Michelle came out, and we settled in. Both our families would come out often and visit with us. They loved that we were in Oak Park and away from the south side. My son Samuel would come out and bring the twins Korey and Kasey; he would barbecue out back of the building. We'd have such a great time. Michelle was really happy.

James had since started his own family and had moved away to Minnesota. He would come up every so often and visit with us and would send for his mom on holidays. I was invited too, but by now, besides managing and maintaining Sam's building, I had got another job with a resale shop in Oak Park. It was called the Economy Shop. So I wasn't able to travel with her. She always had a great time there with her grandchildren. It made me happy to see her happy and know that I wouldn't let anything disappoint her again, especially not me.

Well, everything was going well. Michelle really felt good about living in Oak Park. Then one day, Michelle became a little ill. She was admitted to the Provident Hospital on the south side. She was there for a week or so. When she was released, she was okay. But later, one day, as she and I were in our place, she complained that her tongue was swelling, and she was having difficulty breathing. I took a look and saw that her tongue had swollen at the back of her mouth so you couldn't see the back of her throat. I called 911, and she was rushed to Rush Oak Park Hospital. She was taken right away, and after a while, a doctor came out and told me that I had gotten her there just in time, and had it been any later, it could've been fatal.

They wheeled her out. She had a smile on her face. They had performed an emergency tracheotomy on her. She was fine now. They instructed me on the care she would need from me between doctor's visits. Everything was good. She had gotten used to having it, and I had gotten used to caring for her with it. We went on about our normal routines until, sometime later, she developed difficulty breathing and needed oxygen. Besides that, we were okay.

We continued visiting with family, attending functions, going grocery shopping, and doing everything we were used to doing. Later, my job needed to hire another worker, so I got my cousin Johnny hired. Johnny and I were very close; he would come often and visit with Michelle and myself and I would visit with him often and sometimes stay overnight. Michelle didn't mind, especially if I had, had one cocktail too many. Johnny and I actually had fun at the job and couldn't wait to get there to be around each other. Everyone, bosses included, really took to Johnny in a specially acceptable way. Johnny had a heart condition that would sometimes limit him. But he would try to perform his job anyway until one of the bosses would tell him to just sit the day out and rest. Anytime Johnny would take days off, it was, "How's Johnny doing?" Not focusing on days missed no matter how long he was off!

Then one day at the job, he didn't look well at all to me. I encouraged him to go home and asked if I could go with him. They agreed, but Johnny wouldn't have it. He relaxed for a couple of hours and was on his way home. I kept calling his phone but wasn't getting an answer. So I called his older brother David and then his twin Robert. Later that night, I got a call that Johnny had passed away. It hit me and his coworkers and the employers very hard. The job was closed on the day of his funeral in his honor, and everyone attended, even the customers who knew him. It was some time before I fully recuperated from the loss. One thing that made a bright spot in this for me was that since David and I had come back from Israel and he still had a sister and niece there, he always talked of going there to see them and, definitely, ride on a camel. His desire was fulfilled before his parting. It really gladdened my heart that he had fulfilled that. This funeral wasn't just standing room only. It was just impossible to get inside at all or even pass on the sidewalk on that side of the street. He was that loved by so many.

Michelle and I had moved into an apartment building down the street on Chicago Avenue—a very nice three and a half room apartment. The area was very convenient. I could even walk to my job in twenty minutes. Michelle loved it. All of the windows faced the same way: Chicago Avenue, busy during the day and pin drop quiet during the night. What more could I ask for? We were comfortable and happy. My sons were here in the States doing well on their own, no problems to speak of. Samuel and Yakeen were living in Champaign, Illinois, around their Aunt Barbara. Melvin Jr. had moved to Akron, Ohio. We all communicated almost daily. This was heaven for me. There wasn't anything that could dampen my spirit or so I thought.

But one day, as I sat at home enjoying a quiet evening after work, Michelle and I were playing her favorite card game, gin rummy 500, and then the phone rang. It was one of my sons calling to tell me that Melvin Jr. had been shot and killed in Ohio. Already, he had made a few resentful there among some of the very young guys who had grown up with him in Israel because he had successfully started up a very good and prosperous car cleaning business that rivaled theirs. But the killing itself happened about a dog that he was given charge to watch for someone, and someone else who was involved with that person wanted to take the dog away. An argument ensued; the person left, and Melvin, not being afraid, remained where he was with other friends, and the other person returned with a gun and shot him down.

I called Ohio to get the full story, and I was told the exact same thing my son had told me. The authorities did catch the individual and kept the family up-to-date on the progress of the case. The family arranged to have his body shipped back to Chicago for burial. The service was packed with family and friends of the family and some who had once lived in Israel with us when I lived there. Carolyn flew in. We sat together and consoled each other. We hadn't actually seen each other for many years before now. She wasn't going to be staying in the States. And we still had our daughter Yeef-ah back in Israel who, by this time, had grown up, married, and started her own family.

After a few weeks, Carolyn went back, but we stayed in communication even more than before. She would even still come back now and then on business for the nation but never forgetting to stop in and check on our sons and even see me sometimes. I found that things never really get back to normal; they just get lighter to bear.

Well, it was again back to the routine of things for me. Things were going well at the job. Michelle was going good until, one day, she called me at the job and had a problem with the machine used to supply her oxygen. I went right home and fixed the situation. But that evening, she had some breathing complications. I had done everything that I had been instructed to do by her doctors, but she didn't get better. I took her to the emergency room; she was admitted. They administered to her, and she was supposed to see her trachea doctor, but he wasn't at the hospital. And since she seemed better, she was sent home with a prescription that evening, and the rest of the night, she was fine.

The next morning, she complained of not being able to breathe good. I removed her outer trachea and cleaned it as always, but she was still having difficulty breathing. She would never let me remove the inner one that the doctor always removed and replaced. I couldn't force her to let me even though she knew I knew how. She often suffered anxiety attacks at times. I didn't want to excite her, so I went to the kitchen and made some hot tea. She drank it and seemed to do a little better. I then went to fill her prescription. When I left, she was in the bedroom. But when I returned, she was in the living room. When I entered the door, she just stared at me with a bewildered look in her eyes. She was silent and reached out and grabbed my hand and squeezed it. I took the outer trachea out. But she just slumped over into my chest. I raised her back up and dialed 911. I felt her chest for a heartbeat; there wasn't one. I begged her to please wake up. I prayed and prayed. The paramedics finally came after about ten minutes or so. They got her heart to beating. I was relieved somewhat, but it was painful to see her lying there as she was. There were three paramedics, so I couldn't ride in the ambulance with her. But the police officer who was on the scene who I knew (her name was Christine) offered me a ride to the hospital in her squad car.

When we arrived, I had to wait in the waiting area; not long after, a chaplain came out toward me. I prayed harder and harder and cried. People stared, but I didn't care. He asked if he could pray with me. I agreed; we sat together for a few minutes, then a nurse came out and took me to the back where she was; she was on a ventilator. I knew then the outcome couldn't be good. I called James and one of her sisters, and we stayed for hours until we had to leave and come back the next day when she would be moved upstairs to an ICU area.

They dropped me home. I stayed awake most of the night. The hospital was calling me off and one with questions about her that only I could answer. But each time the phone rang, I prayed it would be a message that she had awakened. The next day, they had moved her. We all went up and the rest of the family came into town to be together. We all went every day.

I went to work for a few days hoping to stay busy and remain optimistic. But my employers felt that I should spend that time with her. They sent their get well wishes daily. We all prayed, cried, and laughed about the good times. Then the word came that we had to make that dreaded decision. It was left to James and myself. It was hard, but it was more for her than ourselves. She was gone, and I had to go on without the joy of her being in my life.

The service was full with family and friends from everywhere. My family also attended. Her family was and always had been supportive and appreciative of me. I recall that she had said to me long before she got sick that she wanted me to look after James if anything should happen to her and treat him like my own son. I promised I would. Her family had always considered me family. Even now, they are always checking on my well-being. And for the first time, I got a chance to go to Minnesota to see what made her so happy being there with James, his wife, Alicia, and the children. So one Christmas holiday, they sent me a round trip ticket to come up and spend the entire holiday season with the family; what a great time I had with my son, my daughter-in-law, and my grandchildren. Now Michelle's family was also my family—brothers, sisters, nieces, and nephews too.

At first, I thought I would move from the apartment to maybe a one room place because now I didn't need all of that space for just me. I packed up the whole apartment. The only things visible were the appliance that belonged to the building and two televisions, one in the living room and one in the bedroom. Only thing not disturbed was the bed and the couch, the floors and walls were bare and boxed. It looked like a storage place. Boxes piled up almost to the ceiling. I had put in applications for places but never followed through when I would be approved for one. This continued for months and months. Then I realized that I really didn't want to leave because this was our love nest, and there were nothing but good memories here. And I shouldn't run from them. I was alone, yes but lonely, no; every time I thought of her, I would smile or laugh to myself picturing the moments. So now I had to unpack the whole apartment and put it back just as it was. It was toilsome, but I enjoyed every minute and didn't think of wanting help.

I went back to work. For a while, I was buying frozen dinners and eating out. Then I said, "What am I doing? I can cook." With what I learned from my grandma and Michelle, there was no excuse for me eating out. I began to cook my Sunday dinners and holiday meals. There was just me but keeping tradition, I always made enough in case someone came by. It was home sweet home.

Before I knew it, five years had passed since Michelle's passing. I was doing so well alone I hadn't given thought to dating anybody and settling down again. I was socializing here and there for the company but not companionship. I enjoyed the company of quite a few other ladies, but the attraction hadn't been strong enough for me to relentlessly pursue any of them. There were many opportunities. I had one coworker who I had become very good friends and I had become friends with his family as well. One day, one of his sisters asked if she could come over to my apartment just to sit and socialize. I agreed. She asked if she could bring a friend. I also agreed. She came and brought her friend with her whose name was Gladys. We sat and talked about my experience in Israel. They were admiring my collection of African art all around the living room. Gladys became very much interested to know more about my life in Israel and my outlook on certain things pertaining to African culture. Christine, being somewhat outspoken, said to me aloud that Gladys was looking for a man. Gladys looked shocked at what she had said. The evening was coming to a close, and Christine had to get back home, and Gladys was driving her. They got up to leave, then Gladys asked if she could come back? And would the hour be too late? I told her that she could, and I would be up late. But I told her she should have my phone number in case she got lost, and she gave me her number too.

They left, and Gladys came back as promised. This time, we talked more about each other personally. Then I felt that she was surely as interested in me as I was in her. The way she reserved herself and selectively asked questions and the way she was poised when she sat across the room from me. She has the air of a very intelligent and strong woman. This was the woman I would want to go on with. We talked until very late, but then she respected I had to go to work the next morning, so she left and promised to call me the next day. She did. Then she would come by every other day. She worked nearby. She was a CNA, then she told me she was having problems with her shower and plumbing at her apartment and asked if she could sometimes come and shower at my place; I agreed.

Later, we began dating. And she would come and spend the night sometimes, and sometimes I would spend nights at her place. We began to spend lots of time together going on weekend getaways. She still would have lots of questions for me about my life in Israel. And a lot of it, she just couldn't believe that I had actually lived there for thirteen years and actually spoke different languages and had multiple wives.

One day, she and I went out to the Hibachi Grill to eat, and she began to research my birth name, my Hebrew name, and the community in Dimona, Israel; she was shocked and so was I that an Israeli I had met in Israel and had told her about had written a book, and I was one of his main subjects. It revealed some of the same things I had told her about. She was stunned. Although the author Haim Chertok had certainly embellished quite a bit about me. I had given him an interview for an Israeli newspaper and had no idea he was going to put me in a book. Upon learning this, Gladys encouraged me to write my own life story. She was right. It was time I should, and besides letting my story be told, I would be leaving a legacy for my children and their children. Gladys, not only because of the book but also in many other aspects of life, had become a great inspiration to me.

Gladys didn't drink or smoke and had been a member of the Jehovah's Witness organization. But she never once attempted to convince me to accept any of their belief. I respected her deeply for that. As I drank occasionally, but she never objected to my drinking. If she did, I couldn't tell. We were definitely opposites but were yet so much alike in many positive ways. She was such a positive force for me that I didn't want to ever disappoint her in any way, big or small.

I later quit drinking completely and geared my energies toward maintaining a healthier lifestyle to become a better and well-rounded man for her and to extend my longevity for my children and grand-children. I had always been one who when I set my mind and heart to do something, I manage to do it without intervention other than my self-will and God's help.

All in all, I came through my experiences unscathed, wiser, more knowledgeable, and, overall, blessed by it. Now that I understand the reasons and purpose, I have no regrets.

ABOUT THE AUTHOR

Melvin Coleman was born on the west side of Chicago on July 12, 1951, to Ossie and Edward Coleman. He was raised on the south side of Chicago and one of eight children.

At an early age, he left home, struggled, hustled, and fought to survive the wilds of the streets. He was always determined to win at any situation that confronted him, never accepting things just as it is but having to always know how and why.

Please leave your review
on amazon + Barnes Noble
Thank you!

CPSIA information can be obtained
at www.ICGtesting.com
Printed in the USA
JSHW032202220322
24149JS00002B/141